BIBLE BELIEVER'S ARCHAEOLOGY

VOLUME 2
THE SEARCH FOR TRUTH

JOHN ARGUBRIGHT

Copyright © 2013 by John Argubright

Bible Believer's Archaeology Volume 2
The Search For Truth
by John Argubright

Printed in the United States of America

ISBN: 978-0-9792148-4-4 (2nd Edition)
(Previously 1rst edition ISBN 1-591604-07-9) 2003

All rights reserved. No part of this publication may be reproduced or transmitted in any form or by any means without written permission of the publisher.

Unless otherwise indicated, Bible quotations are taken from The Holy Bible, New King James Version. Copyright © 1962 by Thomas Nelson, Inc. Also quoted: New International Version Copyright © 1973, 1978, 1984 by International Bible Society. Copyright © 1986 Zondervan Publishing House

This book is copyrighted to protect its misuse and to safeguard the rights of any author, publisher, or individual whose data may have been used in research for this book and to preserve the integrity of quotes from historical sources.

The majority of the historical quotes used in this book were re-translated by the author in an effort to not infringe upon the copyright of others and to protect the authors and publishers of the original source translations.

This book as well as our first and third volumes in the series may be ordered at "BibleHistory.net" as well as from other major online book distributors.

FOUR THINGS GOD WANTS YOU TO KNOW

1. You are a sinner and cannot save yourself.

For all have sinned and fall short of the glory of God.
Romans 3:23

2. God loves and values you so much, He made a way for you to be saved. (Jesus)

"For God so loved the world that He gave His only begotten Son, that whoever believes in Him should not perish but have everlasting life." John 3:16

3. You must repent, Turn to Christ and turn away from your sins. Confess them and forsake them.

If we confess our sins, He is faithful and just to forgive us our sins and to cleanse us from all unrighteousness. 1 John 1:9

4. There is a Heaven and there is a Hell. Where will you spend your Eternity?

"He who believes in the Son has everlasting life; and he who does not believe the Son shall not see life, but the wrath of God abides on him." John 3:36

Introduction

All men and women sometime during their lives will seek after meaning, purpose and truth. For many, their search will bring them to the pages of the Bible and to feet of the gentle carpenter from Nazareth.

But one of the first questions people have is, "Can I really trust the Bible? This book answers the question.

Come along on a journey back in time and watch the historical events of the Bible unfold before your very eyes.

Evidences have been compiled from a variety of sources found outside of the Bible, evidences that prove the accuracy of Scripture.

Read what early historians had to say about Jesus Christ as well as other New Testament figures such as Pontius Pilate, Tiberius Caesar, Quirinius, Herod the Great, the high priest Annas and others.

The events and men of the Old Testament are also revealed in the pages of archaeology. Evidences are provided for The Flood, The Tower of Babel, The Ark of the Covenant, King Cyrus, King Jehu, King Uzziah, Manasseh son of Hezekiah, King Ahaz, the prophet Jeremiah's enemy, and many others.

About the Author:

John Argubright is a researcher and author of the three volume series, *Bible Believer's Archaeology*, as well as the creator of the popular website, BibleHistory.net.

Table of Contents

THE BIRTH OF JESUS	Page 1
QUIRINIUS	Page 6
THE CLEANSING OF THE TEMPLE	Page 14
PONTIUS PILATE	Page 19
THE CRUCIFIED PROPHET	Page 26
AQUILA AND PRISCILLA FLEE FROM ROME	Page 29
THE FAMINE OF ACTS CHAPTER 11	Page 32
THE MARTYRS	Page 36
ACTS 21 - THE EGYPTIAN	Page 41
WALL SEPARATING JEWS AND GENTILES	Page 46
THE FLOOD AND THE TOWER OF BABEL	Page 48
THE ROCK CITY	Page 56
LOT'S DESCENDANTS	Page 63
JEHU & HAZAEL	Page 66
KING UZZIAH	Page 69
AHAZ, KING OF JUDAH	Page 72
SARGON, KING OF ASSYRIA	Page 74
MANASSEH, SON OF HEZEKIAH	Page 77
JEREMIAH'S ENEMY	Page 81

Table of Contents

KING CYRUS OF PERSIA   Page 85

THE ARK OF THE COVENANT   Page 92

SOURCES   Page 99

THE BIRTH OF JESUS

Every year as December 25th rolls around, our minds begin to focus on the birth of that little baby born at Bethlehem. But more than just a baby. The Savior, Christ the Lord.

Throughout the ages many evidences have surfaced which confirm that wonderful event, God becoming man.

One such evidence comes from an early Church leader named Origen. He wrote that the actual cave where Jesus was born could be seen by anyone wanting to visit it. He wrote the following in "Against Celsus," Volume I, chapter 51:

"In regards to the birth of Jesus in Bethlehem, if anyone, after studying Micah's prophecy and the history recorded in the Scriptures, written by the disciples of Jesus, needs to have additional sources of evidence, let him be aware that the Scriptures are confirmed and the Gospel involving His birth. For one can visit the cave located in Bethlehem where He was born, and see the manger where He was wrapped in swaddling-clothes. And this site is talked about with great interest in all the surrounding countries. Even among the enemies of our faith it is being said that in this cave Jesus was born, the One who is worshiped and revered by the Christians."

Even the early Church historians give evidences for the virgin birth. Justin Martyr, who lived around 150 A.D., wrote that if anyone questioned the virgin birth of Jesus, they should go and refer to the official Roman archives of Augustus Caesar.

Another early Church leader was a man by the name of Ignatius. He was brought up under the Apostle John's instruction. In one of his epistles to the Ephesians, which was written sometime around 110 A.D., he made the following statements regarding the Virgin birth:

"Jesus Christ our God was . . . conceived in Mary's womb . . . according to the Holy Spirit. Mary's virginity and the One whom she brought forth . . . these are the mysteries which are commonly known throughout the entire world. Yet these things were done secretly by God."

In 125 A.D. another early writer by the name of Aristides also mentioned the miraculous birth of the Savior.

"He being the Son of God Most High, made known by the Holy Spirit, came down from above, and being born of a Hebrew virgin He took on flesh . . ."

Justin Martyr, wrote these words around 150 A.D.:

"The Lord Jesus Christ our instructor, who was the first born of God the Father, was not born through sexual relations . . . God's power came upon the virgin, lighting upon her while she was still a virgin, causing her to conceive . . . By the will of God, His Son, Jesus Christ was born of the virgin Mary."

According to the Bible, shortly after Jesus was born in Bethlehem, Herod the Great was visited by Magi from the East. They were searching for the King whose Star had risen.

Herod, troubled by this King whom he considered a threat to his imperial reign, sent for the priests to find out where He was to be born. They told him the Child would be born in Bethlehem. Herod then sent his soldiers to that town to slay all the male children two years old and under.

This event may have been alluded to by a non-Christian writer named Ambrosius Macrobius, who around 430 A.D. wrote the following in his work Saturnalia Volume II chapter 4:11:

'While listening amongst the male children's bones, who in Syria king Herod of the Jews had ordered killed, those who were younger then two years of age, his son in like manner he also had slaughtered.' He (Augustus Caesar) says: "It is better to live as Herod's pig than to be his son"

(Note: Syria, at this time, was known as the area between Asia Minor and Egypt, which included Syria, Lebanon and the land of Israel.)

Other pieces of historical evidence confirm the evil character of Herod the Great in keeping with the Biblical record.

Josephus, writing in the first century, recorded that Herod had a number of Torah scholars burned alive for removing Rome's golden eagles from the Temple gates. He also had his wife and a few of his sons murdered simply for considering them a threat to his royal throne.

Fearing that nobody would mourn his death, he also ordered that men, numbering in the thousands, should be locked inside the hippodrome at Jericho and be massacred when he died. This would assure that there would be great mourning on the day of his departure from this world. Luckily, for those concerned, that order was never carried out.

THE GREATEST STATEMENT MADE ABOUT THE BIRTH OF JESUS

"And you, O (tower of the flock) the stronghold of the daughter of Zion, to you shall it come, even the former dominion shall come, the kingdom of the daughter Jerusalem." . . . "But you Bethlehem Ephrathah. Though you are little among the thousands of Judah, yet out of you shall come forth to Me The One to be Ruler in Israel, Whose goings forth are from of old, from everlasting."
Micah 4:8-5:2

In Micah 4:8, the Hebrew word for "Tower of the Flock" is "Migdal Eder." Located near Bethlehem today is a little spot considered to be the ancient site of Migdal Eder.

You see, our Lord Jesus was born in Bethlehem where all sacrificial lambs were born, and our Lord Jesus died in Jerusalem where all sacrificial lambs were killed.

"The good shepherd lays down his life for the sheep."

John 10:11

New Testament   Chapter 2

QUIRINIUS

Each year during Christmas, millions of believers in churches all around the world read of the birth of Jesus from the Gospel account as recorded in Luke chapter two. And each year the man who governed in Syria at the time of our Lord's first coming is also mentioned. His name is Quirinius, or if you have a King James Version of the Bible, Cyrenius.

History records much of the man who was lucky enough to be associated with the birth of our Savior. The earliest historical account we have of Quirinius comes from an inscription found in Antioch Pisidia known as Res Gestae, 'The Deeds of Augustus Caesar by Augustus'. The inscription places him as consul in 12 B.C. This position was attained by only two prominent Romans every year and they governed as the Roman heads of state. The inscription reads as follows:

"A great crowd of people came together from all over Italy to my election, more then had ever gathered before in Rome, when **Publius Sulpicius** (Quirinius) **and Gaius Valgius were consuls."**

(Res Gestae 10)

Quirinius was by no means a small figure in Roman politics or in his association with the Emperors of Rome. So respected was Quirinius to the Caesar's that upon his death in 22 A.D. the Emperor Tiberius honored him before the entire Senate. The following is his tribute as recorded by the Roman historian Tacitus:

"Around this time, he (Tiberius Caesar) requested that the Senate pay tribute to the death of **Sulpicius Quirinius with a public funeral . . . A tireless soldier, who had by his faithful services** become consul during the reign of Augustus, and later was honored for his victory concerning his assault on the fortresses of the Homonadenses in Cilicia** (The province of Cilicia is located just northwest of neighboring Syria.) **Later he was appointed to be an adviser to Caius Caesar in the government of Armenia** (Caius was the son of Augustus who was sent to administer Syria as an Imperial Legate around 1 B.C., He was then wounded in nearby Armenia in 3 A.D. and later died the following year.) **as well as being an advisor to Tiberius, when he was at Rhodes** (the Island just off the coast of Asia to which Tiberius was exiled somewhere between 6 B.C. and 2 A.D.) **The Roman emperor spoke of these things before the entire Senate, and praised Quirinius for his excellent service**, while he criticized Marcus Lollius, whom he blamed for teaching Caius Caesar the traits of being disobedient and divisive. But most of the citizens were not fond of the memory of **Quirinius**, because of his involvement in the events surrounding Lepida, whose account I have previously mentioned, as well as the harsh and **dangerous power he held during his last years in office."** Tacitus Annals - Book III

    This account of Tacitus proves that Quirinius was governing militarily in the area of Syria well before becoming the civilian governor of Syria and taking a second census of Judea around 6 A.D., as recorded by the Jewish historian Josephus.

    Another inscription, which surfaced in the late 1600's, known as the Aemilius Secundus inscription, also mentions Quirinius governing in Syria as well as ordering a census. The inscription reads as follows:

    "Quintus Aemilius Secundus, from Palatine, with honors he was decorated in the camp of the divine Augustus under **Publius Sulpicius Quirinius legate of Caesar in Syria**, prefect of the first Augustan cohort, prefect of the navy's second cohort.

Commanded by Quirinius to conduct a census of the district of Apamea's 117,000 citizens; He was also sent by Quirinius to capture the fortresses of the Itureans in the mountains of Lebanon. (Inscriptiones Latinae Selectae #2683)

This inscription shows that the authority of Quirinius in Syria extended to areas south of Syria as well, such as Iturea which lays just north of Galilee.

It also states that Quirinius governed as an Imperial legate from Syria and was thereby given the authority by Rome to conduct any census to be taken in the provinces nearby.

Two other inscriptions were found in the early 1900's in Pisidian Antioch, which served as a military command center and eastern outpost for the Roman Empire. The first inscription reads as follows:

"C. Caristanius C F Sergius Fronto Caesiaus Iulius, perfect of civil engineers, priest, perfect of **P. Sulpicius Quirinius the Duumvir**, Perfect of M. Servilius, from this man and with an edict, a statue was erected with the blessings of the council.

(Inscriptiones Latinae Selectae #9502)

Stone mentioning Quirinius
ILS 9502

The second inscription reads:

"To C. Caristanius Fronto Caesianus Iulius, son of Gaius, from the tribe of Sergia, prefect of civil engineers, military tribune of the twelfth legion, prefect of the Bosporan cohort, priest, prefect of **P. Sulpicius Quirinius**, duumvir, prefect of Marcus Servilius, prefect . . ." (ILS#9503)

Marcus Servilius, who is mentioned alongside Quirinius in these two inscriptions, was Roman consul in 3 A.D. Quirinius is also identified as a duumvir which means he was one of two people that jointly held power.

And even though all these evidences point to Quirinius governing in the region during the Biblical census, many skeptics continue to argue that Rome would not have taxed or conducted a census in Israel before it became a Roman province in 6 A.D.

But Josephus records that the Jews were being taxed by the Romans through their Syrian governors as early as 44 B.C. Josephus writes: "Cassius rode into Syria in order to take command of the army stationed there, and on the Jews he placed a tax of 700 silver talents. Antipater gave the job of collecting this tax to his sons . . ." Jewish Antiquities XIV 271

History also records that just before the birth of our Lord, Judea was being taxed highly under Herod the Great, who was appointed King of Judea by Caesar Augustus, and Herod was subservient to him.

After Herod died, Josephus records the following: "Archelaus grieved over the death of his father for several days and then . . . from his throne of gold, he gave a speech to the crowd . . . pleased by his words, the people immediately began to test his sincerity by requesting certain favors from him. Some pleaded for their yearly taxes to be reduced . . . while others pleaded that he would take away the excessive sales taxes that were being levied on goods being brought and sold."(Jewish Antiquities XVII 200)

He also recorded that the common people hated Herod because of the high tax burden he imposed on them. Josephus states: "The amount of people to whom he lavished his money were very numerous.

And because of this, he was forced to collect it through unjust means. Because Herod was aware that his subjects hated him so much due to these past crimes, he did not think it would make any difference to treat them kindly, for it might harm his revenue; he therefore, knowing that his subjects feared him because of his harshness, continued on in pursuit of financial gain." Antiquities XVI 150-170

To show how much he taxed the people, when he died he left ten million pieces of silver to Augustus Caesar and five million to Caesar's wife Julia and others. (Jewish Antiquities XVII 190)

We also know that Augustus Caesar ordered a census in 8 B.C., this would have taken many years to implement and complete in all the provinces under direct and indirect control of Rome.

The following is an account given by Augustus of the census:

"During my sixth term as consul (28 B.C.), I along with my comrade Marcus Agrippa, commanded a census be taken of the people. I directed a lustrum, the first in forty-one years, in which 4,063,000 Roman citizens were counted. And once again, with imperial authority, I single handedly authorized a lustrum when the consuls of Rome were Gaius Censorinus and Gaius Asinius (8 B.C.), during which time 4,233,000 Roman citizens were counted." (Res Gestae 8 - The Deeds of Augustus by Augustus)

This census in 8 B.C. seems to have occurred to early in history to be considered the Biblical census in which Joseph and Mary were registered. The early church historians Tertullian, Origen, and Eusibius all held that Christ was born in 2 B.C. and that Herod died the following year in 1 B.C.

The earliest manuscripts of "Jewish Antiquities" by Josephus also mention that Herod's son Phillip died in the 22nd year of Tiberius, which would be 36 A.D. and that he ruled for 37 years. Thus giving a date of 1 B.C. for his appointment as Tetrarch right after the death of his father Herod the Great.

The Biblical census was probably implemented by Herod to coincide with Rome's decree that everyone throughout the Empire should give honor to Augustus Caesar. This took place in 2 B.C. when Augustus was given the title "Father of my country" by the Roman Senate and was honored throughout all the empire.

This is recorded in the annals of Caesar who wrote the following: "while I was administering my thirteenth consulship (2 B.C.) the Senate and the equestrian order and the entire Roman people gave me the title "Father of my country" and decreed that this title should be inscribed upon the vestibule of my house and in the senate-house and in the Forum Augustum beneath the quadriga erected in my honor by decree of the senate." (Res Gestae, VI.35)

The Roman historian Suetonius in his work *Life of Augustus*, 58, also mentions that the title "Father of thy country" was given to Augustus. In 59-60 it states: "Many of the provinces, in addition to temples and altars, established games every five years in his honor in almost every one of their towns."

These events in 2 B.C. may have led Herod to place Rome's symbol, a large golden eagle, on the main gate of the Temple to honor Caesar right before Herod's death which probably occurred early in 1 B.C. This, and the oath required by all Israel to honor Caesar, is recorded by Josephus in his book "Antiquities of the Jews" Book 17, Chapters 2 and 6:

"The sect of the Pharisees, who constantly opposed kings with great zeal . . . after the majority of the Jews gave assurance of their good will toward Caesar, as well as to the king's government, these Pharisees, numbering over six thousand, did not swear the oath . . . They were believed to have had foreknowledge of things to come by Divine inspiration, for they had foretold that Herod's government would come to an end . . . Later two leaders who were educated in the law and beloved by the people, Judas and Matthias, incited a mob of young men to tear down the large golden eagle which king Herod had placed over the great gate of the Temple. This violated Jewish law which prohibits an idol of any living thing from being put up in the temple.

These men were arrested and Herod ordered the leaders to be burned alive . . . After this Herod's illness worsened and he began to suffer greatly."

Josephus also mentions that shortly after Herod's death a dispute broke out as to who should take over the rule of Herod's territories. One of the people Caesar asked for an opinion on this issue was from his adopted son Caius, who was being groomed to be the next Caesar. Shortly afterwards Caius was appointed legate in Syria. So if Herod died in 1 B.C. it would correspond with Caius being installed as legate to Syria shortly afterwards.

Since the Bible says Quirinius was governing in Syria at the time of the census, right before Herod's death, it would make sense that Augustus would have chosen him to be the advisor to his son Caius who was being sent to that region.

All these events fit nicely together with what is recorded in the Gospel of Luke. The historian Luke, giving the most accurate account of the census and the one that atheists and infidels refuse to believe, states: **"I myself have carefully investigated everything from the beginning, it seemed good to me to write an orderly account for you . . . In those days Caesar Augustus issued a decree that a census should be taken of the entire Roman world. This was the first census that took place while Quirinius was governing in Syria.**

You see, Caesar, whom the Romans held as

being Divine, though he was only a mere mortal man, took a census to count all the people in his empire. And also to find out and document which ones were citizens of his kingdom and which ones were not.

And one day, the One who is not a mere mortal, but truly God, will hold His own registration.

And each man and woman will appear before Him face to face. And He will open up the Book of Life to see if you are entitled to be called a citizen of His kingdom. A simple record of what you have done with the message of salvation? That message that the Lamb of God shed his blood on a cross, to die in your place.

Do you believe?
Are you registered in the Lamb's book of Life?

THE GREATEST STATEMENTS REGARDING CITIZENSHIP IN HEAVEN:

He was in the world, and though the world was made through Him, the world did not recognize Him, He came to His own, but His own did not receive Him. Yet to all who do receive, to all who believe in His name, He gave the right to be called **Children of God.** John 1:10-12

For many walk, of whom I have told you often, and now tell you even weeping, that they are the enemies of the cross of Christ: whose end is destruction, whose god is their belly, and whose glory is in their shame; who set their mind on earthly things. **For our citizenship is in heaven**, from which we also eagerly wait for the Savior, the Lord Jesus Christ, who will transform our lowly body that it may be conformed to His glorious body, according to the working by which He is able even to subdue all things to Himself. Philippians 3:18-21

CLEANSING OF THE TEMPLE

Now the time of the Passover was near, and Jesus went up to Jerusalem. And He found men in the temple area who were selling cattle and sheep and doves, and also the moneychangers who were doing business. So He fashioned a whip out of cords, and went into the temple and drove out the cattle and the sheep, and he overturned the tables of the money changers and He scattered their coins. And He went up to those who were selling doves and said to them, "Get these things out of here! How dare you turn My Father's house into a marketplace!" Then His disciples remembered what was written in the Scriptures, "Zeal for Your house will consume me."

John 2:13-17

Confirmation that the Temple was being turned into a marketplace during the time of Jesus can be found in some early Jewish writings. First of all, there is a record of the common practice of setting up money changers in the temple area during Passover. The Talmud states the following:

Beginning on the 1st of Adar (the month before Passover), a proclamation was made to the people that they should prepare . . . On the 15th day of Adar, moneychangers were sent out to collect the Half-Shekel for its donation . . . On the 25th day of Adar, moneychangers were installed in the Temple itself to help in the collecting of the Half-Shekel donation: Megillah 29a-b

Not only were the moneychangers robbing the people, but history records that excessive prices were being charged by those who were selling animals used in Temple sacrifice.

For example, according to Leviticus 12:6-8, after an Israelite woman had given birth, she was to bring a sacrifice to the temple, preferably a sheep. But if she was poor and could not afford the price of a sheep, she could take two doves or two pigeons for the sacrifice, one for a burnt offering and one for a sin offering. The Jewish Mishna states that because of their greed, those who were selling birds rose their prices so much that the poorer woman of the community could not afford them. Rabban Shimon ben Gamaliel the Elder, a leading rabbi of his time and a descendant of Gamaliel, whom the Bible says trained the apostle Paul as a pharisee before Paul had come to Christ, took immediate action to lower the market price. The Mishna gives this account in Kritut 1:7:

"If a woman had given birth five times during her life . . . after she brings a single sacrifice, she will be able to eat sanctified foods once again. But she is still under an oath to bring four more. It eventually came to pass that the cost of two birds rose dramatically to one gold zuz. Rabban Shimon ben Gamaliel declared: "I pledge that before I go to bed this very night, the price of birds will fall!" He headed straight to the courtyard and instructed the people to obey the following regulation: "After giving birth five times, a woman . . . needs to bring just one sacrificial offering to cover all five births . . . That very day, the price of birds plummeted to one quarter of a silver zuz."

Even many of the high priests during the first century seemed to have given up their love of God for the love of money. Most notably the High priest whom Jesus was brought before, Annas, along with his five sons who succeeded him to that position. The Temple sacrifice during their reigns can best be summed up by the words "The Marketplace of the family of Annas"

The historian Josephus sheds some light on the actions of one member of this family, Annas the younger, the man who had James (the writer of he book of James in the Bible) stoned to death. Josephus states:

"The high priest, Ananus, (after he had been relieved from his office) to some degree, was respected and feared by the citizens, but in a bad way; for he loved to hoard money. He became good friends with Albinus, and of the newly installed high priest. He did so by offering them bribes; he also had wicked servants, who associated with all sorts of evil men, and went to the thrashing-floors, and took the tithes that belonged to the priests by force, and beat anyone who would not give these tithes to them. So the other high priests that followed him as well as his servants acted likewise without anyone being able to stop them; so that some of the priests, those who were old and were being supported with those tithes, died for lack of food."

A matter of fact, Jewish history records that these High priests who walked the temple courts during the first century were despised by the majority of the people for their brutality and hunger for money. So much so that there is a strong condemnation of these men in the Talmud.

Tosefta, Menachoth 13.21 states a Rabbinic Lament over the brutality of the Sadducees. It says:
"Abba Saul ben Betnith and Abba Jose ben Johanan of Jerusalem say:"

"Woe to the house of Boethus! Woe to me because of their rods!" (Simon, son of Boethus, was father in-law to Herod. He was a high priest during the reign of Herod the Great. Shortly after Simon died, Eleazar and Joazar, who were also the sons of Boethus, became high priests.)

"Woe to the house of Qadros (Cantheros)! Woe to me because of their pens!" (Simon Cantheros was one of the high priests appointed during the rule of Herod Agrippa)

"Woe to the house of Elhanan, woe to the house of whispers!" (Elhanan is translated 'Ananus or Annas' in Greek and here refers to the high priest Annas of the New Testament and his sons.)

"Woe to the house of Elisha! Woe to me because of their pens!"

"Woe to the house of Ishmael ben Phabi! For they are high priests and their sons, treasurers and their sons-in-law who were (temple) officers!" "And their servants came and beat us up with staves!" (Ishmael son of Phabi (Fabus) was a high priest under Valerius Gratus, procurator of Judea. Phabi served as priest for one year from 15-16 A.D. Later, around 56-62 A.D., Ishmael ben Phabi was also appointed as high priest.)

JESUS GREATEST STATEMENT CONCERNING RICHES:

"Whoever desires to come after Me, let him deny himself, and take up his cross, and follow Me. "For whoever desires to save his life will lose it, but whoever loses his life for My sake and the gospel's will save it. **"For what will it profit a man if he gains the whole world, and loses his own soul?** "Or what will a man give in exchange for his soul? "For whoever is ashamed of Me and My words in this adulterous and sinful generation, of him the Son of Man also will be ashamed when He comes in the glory of His Father with the holy angels."

Mark 8:34-38

WHAT GOD THINKS OF THE PROSPERITY GOSPEL:

"If anyone teaches otherwise and does not consent to wholesome words, even the words of our Lord Jesus Christ, and to the doctrine which accords with godliness, **he is proud, knowing nothing, and destitute of the truth, who suppose that godliness is a means of financial gain. From such withdraw yourself.**

Now godliness with contentment is great gain. For we brought nothing into this world, and it is certain we can carry nothing out. And having food and clothing, with these we shall be content."

1Timothy 6:3-8

PONTIUS PILATE

In 1961 an Italian excavation uncovered an inscription bearing the name Pontius Pilate. This was the first physical evidence found outside of the Bible to confirm his existence.

The huge block of limestone which carried the inscription was found at the city of Caesarea and is engraved with the words:

. . . . . . **S TIBERIEVM**	(Tiberieum)
. . *[PO]***NTIVS PILATVS**	(Pontius Pilate)
*[PRA]***ECTVS IVDA***[EA]***E**	(Perfect Judea)

The first word, *Tiberieum*, probably refers to a temple dedicated to the emperor Tiberius.

Pilate's name was also recorded by the well-known Roman historian, Cornelius Tacitus, who mentioned that Pilate crucified Christ just as recorded in the Bible. Tacitus, who was born around 52 A.D. and became Governor of Asia in 112 A.D., wrote the following in his History:

"Nothing which could be done by man, nor any amount of treasure that the prince could give, nor all the sacrifices which could be presented to the gods, could clear Nero from being believed to have ordered the burning, the fire of Rome. So to silence the rumor, he tortured and falsely charged those who were called the Christians, who were hated for their large following. **Christus, the founder of the name, was executed by Pontius Pilate, the Judean procurator, during the rule of Tiberius.**"

Some ancient writers also believed that Pilate sent a report back to Rome of the trial of Jesus. For example, around 150 A.D., Justin Martyr, writing in his defense of Christianity (First Apology) which he sent to the Roman Emperor Antoninus Pius, directed him to Pilate's report which he believed existed somewhere in the imperial archives:

"The statement, "They spiked my hands and my feet" he says, are they not an accurate portrayal of the nails that were fixed in His hands and His feet on the cross, and after He was executed, those who crucified Him cast lots and divided His clothing amongst themselves; these things did occur, and you may find them in the **'Acts' recorded under Pontius Pilate**."

Later on he says: "At His coming the lame shall leap, tongue's that stammer shall speak clearly, the blind shall see, and the lepers shall be cleansed, and the dead shall rise and walk about. And you can learn that he did all these things from the **Acts of Pontius Pilate**."

According to other historians, Pilate is portrayed as being a very cruel man. Philo of Alexandria, who wrote around 40 A.D. and was a contemporary of Jesus, had this to say about Pilate in his work entitled *"The embassy to Gaius 299-305"*:

"An official by the name of Pilate was appointed to be prefect of Judea. Rather then honoring Tiberius, he caused trouble amongst the Jews. In Herod's palace, in the Holy City, he installed gilded shields. They were inscribed with no image or anything that was forbidden, except for a small inscription, which stated two things, the name of the one in whose honor it was dedicated and the name of the person who commanded it to be installed.

But when this became widely known amongst the Jews, they appealed to the four sons of King

Herod, who were held in high respect and were treated as if they were kings. They urged Pilate to remove the shields, and not to violate their customs as other kings and emperors had previously done.

Pilate was a proud man who was both stubborn and cruel, he refused their demands. But they cried out even louder: "Do not cause a war! Or a revolt by our people! Let the peace between us stand! To dishonor our long held traditions will bring no honor to the emperor. Do not insult our nation and bring dishonor to Tiberius. He does not approve of your doing away with our traditions. If you say that he does, show us some letter or decree, so that we may stop appealing to you and go to our master by means of an ambassador."

On hearing this, Pilate became frightened, for he knew that if they really went to the Emperor they would also report on how he had been governing, fearing they would accuse him, and justly so, of cruelty, violence, thefts, assaults, executing prisoners without a trial, and many other harsh acts.

Pilate then became angry and apprehensive, he did not know which way to turn, for he had neither the courage to remove what he had done, nor the desire to do anything which would please those under his rule. But at the same time he knew that Tiberius would not approve of his behavior. Pilate tried to conceal his emotions, but when the Jewish officials saw that he was regretting what he had done, they in return wrote a letter to Tiberius, pleading their case as forcibly as they knew how.

Tiberius was furious and wrote back to Pilate rebuking him with great threats! This was unusual, for he (Caesar) was not easily moved to anger but let his actions speak for themselves.

Immediately, and without delay, he wrote back to Pilate, using an untold number of harsh words to rebuke him for his arrogance and pride and ordered him to remove the shields at once and to have them sent back to the seaport of Caesarea . . . , there they were to be placed in the temple of Augustus. This was promptly done.

In this way both the honor of the emperor and the policy of Rome towards Jerusalem remained in place.

Pilate's fear of a rebuke from Tiberius Caesar can also be found in the gospel of John chapter 19 verses 6-14:

Pilate said to them, "You take Him and crucify Him, for I find no fault in Him." The Jews answered him, "We have a law, and according to our law He ought to die, because He made Himself the Son of God."

Therefore, when Pilate heard that saying, he was the more afraid, and went again into the Praetorium, and said to Jesus, "Where are You from?" But Jesus gave him no answer.

Then Pilate said to Him, "Are You not speaking to me? Do You not know that I have power to crucify You, and power to release You?"

Jesus answered, "You could have no power at all against Me unless it had been given you from above. Therefore the one who delivered Me to you has the greater sin."

From then on Pilate sought to release Him, but the Jews cried out, saying, "If you let this Man go, you are not Caesar's friend."

"Whoever makes himself a king speaks against Caesar." **When Pilate therefore heard that saying**, he brought Jesus out and sat down in the judgment seat in a place that is called The Pavement, but in Hebrew, Gabbatha. Now it was the Preparation Day of the Passover, and about the sixth hour. And he said to the Jews, "Behold your King!"

Another historian, Flavius Josephus, also wrote an account which mentioned Pilate:

"On another occasion he caused a riot by spending the sacred treasure from the temple, without permission, on the construction of an aqueduct which brought water into the city from a distance of seventy kilometers away. Mad with rage at this proceeding, the crowd formed a ring around the tribunal of Pilate, who was visiting Jerusalem at the time, and attacked him with a violent outburst.

He foreseeing a revolt beforehand, had dispatched among the crowd a troop of his soldiers, disguised as civilians but armed, with orders not to use their swords but to beat any rioter who got out of hand. At the proper time he motioned to his men.

The Jews perished in large numbers, some from the blows which they had received, while others were trampled to death by the crowds who were trying to flee from the beatings. Frightened by the sight of the victims, the multitude grew silent." *The Jewish War 2.175-177*

It is possible that Jesus may have alluded to this event in the gospel of Luke 13:1-3 which says:

"There were present at that season some who told Him about the **Galileans whose blood Pilate had mingled with their sacrifices**. And Jesus answered and said to them, "Do you suppose that these Galileans were worse sinners than all other Galileans, because they suffered such things?"

"I tell you, no; but unless you repent you will all likewise perish."

The Bible in John 18:33-38 states: Then Pilate entered the Praetorium again, called Jesus, and said to Him, "Are You the King of the Jews?"

Jesus answered him, "Are you speaking for yourself about this, or did others tell you this concerning Me?" Pilate answered, "Am I a Jew? Your own nation and the chief priests have delivered You to me. What have You done?"

Jesus answered, "My kingdom is not of this world. If My kingdom were of this world, My servants would fight, so that I should not be delivered to the Jews; but now My kingdom is not from here."

Pilate therefore said to Him, "Are You a king then?"

Jesus answered, "You say rightly that I am a king. For this cause I was born, and for this cause I have come into the world, that I should bear witness to the truth. Everyone who is of the *truth* hears My voice." Pilate said to Him, "*What is truth?*" And when he had said this, he went out again to the Jews, and said to them, "I find no fault in Him at all."

THE ANSWER OF JESUS CONCERNING WHAT IS TRUTH:

Jesus said to him, "I am the way, the **Truth**, and the life. No one comes to the Father except through Me. "If you had known Me, you would have known My Father also; and from now on you know Him and have seen Him." John 14:6-7

THE CRUCIFIED PROPHET

During the second century A.D., in one of his ancient works, a Greek writer by the name of Lucian makes reference to Jesus. And although Lucian was a man who opposed Christ, and that is evident in his writing, he does acknowledge that Jesus was crucified, that Christians worship Him as God, that they do so based on faith alone, and believe that they have eternal life through Him.

Lucian writes: "As you are aware, the Christians worship the man to this very day - He being well known for establishing their unusual form of worship, and for that reason he was crucified . . . . You see, these men begin with the notion that they will be immortal for all eternity, which explains why they do not fear death and is why they give themselves over to his worship; and it was also taught by this lawgiver that they are all brothers, from the very second that they begin to follow him, and they turn their backs on the gods in Greece, and worship this crucified prophet, and live according to his commands. They believe all this purely by faith alone. As a result, worldly goods mean nothing to them and they treat it as property to be used among themselves for the common good."

MOSES FIRST WROTE CONCERNING THIS PROPHET:

"And the LORD said to me: 'What they have spoken is good. 'I will raise up for them a Prophet like you from among their brethren, and will put My words in His mouth, and He shall speak to them all that I command Him. 'And it shall be that whoever will not hear My words, which He speaks in My name, I will require it of him."

Deuteronomy 18:17-19

THE GREATEST WORDS SPOKEN BY THIS PROPHET:

On the last day, that great day of the feast, Jesus stood and cried out, saying, "If anyone thirsts, let him come to Me and drink. "He who believes in Me, as the Scripture has said, out of his heart will flow rivers of living water." But this He spoke concerning the Spirit, whom those believing in Him would receive; for the Holy Spirit was not yet given, because Jesus was not yet glorified.
Therefore many from the crowd, when they heard this saying, said, "Truly this is the Prophet."

John 7:37-40

THE GREATEST PROPHECY GIVEN ABOUT THIS CRUCIFIED PROPHET:

My God, My God, why have You forsaken Me? . . . All those who see Me ridicule Me; They shoot out the lip, they shake the head, saying, "He trusted in the LORD, let Him rescue Him; Let Him deliver Him, since He delights in Him!" . . . I am poured out like water, And all My bones are out of joint; My heart is like wax; It has melted within Me. My strength is dried up like a potsherd, And My tongue clings to My jaws; You have brought Me to the dust of death. For dogs have surrounded Me; The congregation of the wicked has enclosed Me. They pierced My hands and My feet;

"I can count all My bones. They look and stare at Me. They divide My garments among them, And for My clothing they cast lots . . . I will declare Your name to My brethren; In the midst of the assembly I will praise You. You who fear the LORD, praise Him! All you descendants of Jacob, glorify Him, And fear Him, all you offspring of Israel! For He has not despised nor abhorred the affliction of the afflicted; Nor has He hidden His face from Him; But when He cried to Him, He heard. My praise shall be of You in the great assembly; I will pay My vows before those who fear Him. The poor shall eat and be satisfied; Those who seek Him will praise the LORD. Let your heart live forever! All the ends of the world Shall remember and turn to the LORD, And all the families of the nations Shall worship before You. For the kingdom is the Lord's, And He rules over the nations. All the prosperous of the earth Shall eat and worship; All those who go down to the dust Shall bow before Him, Even he who cannot keep himself alive. A posterity shall serve Him. It will be recounted of the Lord to the next generation, They will come and declare His righteousness to a people who will be born, That He has done this."

Psalm 22

AQUILA AND PRISCILLA FLEE FROM ROME

In A.D.49, the Roman Emperor Claudius Caesar expelled all Jews from the city of Rome. This account is recorded by Suetonius, a court official who served under the Emperor Hadrian. He wrote a history entitled 'The Life of Claudius' in which he stated the following:

"Because the Jewish people were constantly causing disorders, the catalyst being Chrestus, he expelled them from Rome" (Note: Chrestus may be an alternate spelling for Christos which is the Greek word for Christ.)

This small statement by the Roman historian confirms the Biblical passage found in Acts 18:1-2:

'After these things Paul departed from Athens and went to Corinth. And he found a certain Jew named Aquila, born in Pontus, who had recently come from Italy with his wife Priscilla **because Claudius had commanded all the Jews to depart from Rome**;'

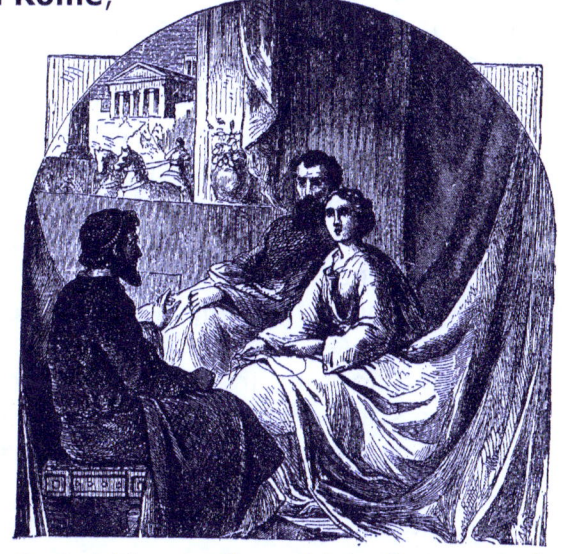

Paul visiting Aquila and Priscilla in Corinth

A letter written by Claudius in 41 A.D. also confirms his hostility toward the Jewish people.

Letter of Emperor Claudius to the Alexandrians in Egypt:

"From Tiberius Claudius Caesar, Imperator, Pontifex Maximus, Holder of the Tribunician Power, Consul Emissary. To the City of the Alexandrians, I send my regards . . .

"To your question, as to whom is responsible for the conflict with the Jews, or should I say our war with them, . . . I have decided not to make a detailed investigation into it. But if any party wishes to renew this violence, they shall see my wrath unfold. May this be my final warning, that unless you put an end to this destructive behavior and hatred toward one another, this tolerant ruler will be forced to display a righteous anger. I say to you once again, that on the one hand, the Alexandrians have shown that they have acted with kindness and respect toward the Jews, who have lived among you for many years. And you have allowed them to worship their God freely, and to observe their customs and traditions just as Augustus Caesar had done previously. And after hearing the arguments from both parties, I have decided to allow their customs to continue; yet I have clearly made it known to the Jews that they are not to ask for any additional freedoms accept those which they already enjoy. They are also to refrain from sending out separate ambassadors, since you and they are both residents of the same city . . . From now on, Jews may no longer migrate to the city by traveling down the river from Syria or Egypt, since this would raise suspicions in my mind as to their reasons for doing so. If my orders are not followed, I will take action against those troublemakers who are infecting the whole world with this plague. But, if you refrain from these ways, and you consent to live with mutual respect and kindness toward one another, I on my part will maintain a peaceful relationship with your city, which has a long-standing tradition of mutual friendship."

THE MINISTRY OF AQUILA AND PRISCILLA TO AN ALEXANDRIAN JEW

'Now a certain Jew named Apollos, born at Alexandria, an eloquent man and mighty in the Scriptures, came to Ephesus. This man had been instructed in the way of the Lord; and being fervent in spirit, he spoke and taught accurately the things of the Lord, though he knew only the baptism of John. So he began to speak boldly in the synagogue.
When Aquila and Priscilla heard him, they took him aside and explained to him the way of God more accurately. And when he desired to cross to Achaia, the brethren wrote, exhorting the disciples to receive him; and when he arrived, he greatly helped those who had believed through grace; for he vigorously refuted the Jews publicly, showing from the Scriptures that Jesus is the Christ.'

Acts 18:24-28

THE FAMINE OF ACTS CHAPTER 11

Another Biblical event confirmed in the pages of history regarding Claudius is found in the book of Acts chapter 11 verses 27-28:

"And in these days prophets came from Jerusalem to Antioch."

"Then one of them, named Agabus, stood up and showed by the Spirit that **there was going to be a great famine throughout all the world, which also happened in the days of Claudius Caesar.**"

The fifth century historian Orosius mentions this famine in Syria which occurred in 46 and 47 A.D. A translation of Orosius was later made by King Alfred of England during the middle ages and was quoted in what are known as "The Anglo-Saxon Chronicles." They give an overview of British history from 1 A.D. to 1154 A.D. and contain the following remarks:

"**A.D. 46:** In this year, Claudius, the second Roman emperor to invade Britain, put much of the island under his control and added the Orkneys to Rome's kingdom. This took place in the fourth year of his rule. **In this same year, a great famine in Syria took place which Luke mentions in his book, "The Acts of the Apostles.**" Due to his incompetence, the Emperor Claudius Nero almost lost control of the British isle.

A.D. 46: In this year, the Emperor Claudius invaded Britain and conquered much of the island. The island of Orkney was also added to his empire.

A.D. 47: In this year, the evangelist Mark began to write his gospel in Egypt.

A.D. 47: During the fourth year of his rule, **there was a great famine in Syria which Luke**

mentions in his book "The Acts of the Apostles."

Other early historians mentioned this famine which extended beyond Israel. Josephus wrote in Antiquities 20 chapter 1.3-2.5: "Herod, the brother of Agrippa who had perished, was allowed to govern over Chalcis. He asked **Claudius Caesar** for control over the temple along with the sacred treasury, and the ability to choose the high priests, and he was given all that he had asked for."

"Around this time lived queen Helena of Adiabene, along with her son Izates. They both began to follow the Jewish way, turning away from their past lifestyle . . . **Her arrival was of great help to the masses in Jerusalem; for there was a famine in the land that overtook them, and many people died of starvation.** When it became necessary to obtain food abroad, queen Helena sent some of her attendants, with money, to the city of Alexandria to purchase as much grain as possible. She also sent others to the island of Cyprus to bring back dried figs. This whole process happened very quickly, and as soon as they had returned, they handed the provisions out to those who were in dire need of them. Because of this, she left behind a legacy and was held in great respect by the people and the nation at large. And when her son Izates **became aware of this famine, he sent a large gift to the leaders in Jerusalem.**"

Suetonius also mentions this famine in 'Life of Claudius' chapter 18: **"There was a scarcity of food, which was the result of bad harvests that occurred during a span of several years."**

Even the Roman historian Tacitus mentions the famine in his Annals, chapter 11:4: "A vision that came to him at night was the reason charges were filed against the man. **In this dream, he claimed** to have seen Claudius crowned with a wreath made of wheat, the ears of which were folded downward. And from this vision, he predicted lean harvests to come."

THE GREATEST FAMINE THAT EVER OCCURRED

"And it shall come to pass in that day," says the Lord GOD, "That I will make the sun go down at noon, And I will darken the earth in broad daylight;

I will turn your feasts into mourning, And all your songs into lamentation; I will bring sackcloth on every waist, And baldness on every head; I will make it like mourning for an only son, And its end like a bitter day.

"Behold, the days are coming," says the Lord GOD, "That I will send a famine on the land, Not a famine of bread, Nor a thirst for water, But of hearing the words of the LORD.

They shall wander from sea to sea, And from north to east; They shall run to and fro, seeking the word of the LORD, But shall not find it. "In that day the fair virgins And strong young men Shall faint from thirst.

Amos 8:9-13

New Testament   Chapter 8

THE MARTYRS

Throughout the world today, thousands of Christians are being persecuted for their faith in Jesus Christ. The same was true for the early church.

One of the earliest accounts of Christian persecution found outside of the Bible comes from two enemies of Christ. Pliny the Younger, the Roman governor of Bithynia in Asia Minor. And the other, the Roman Emperor Trajan. Both men persecuted the early Christians for not worshiping the false gods of Rome.

In a letter dated to around 112 A.D., Pliny wrote the following to the Emperor Trajan:

"It has always been my custom to ask my lord for instructions on all unclear issues. For no one can give me better advice and guidance on matters where I have had no previous experience. Since I have never taken part in the trials of Christians, I would like to know what crimes they should be punished for, should I investigate them, and to what extreme. It is also unclear to me as to whether or not I should treat the young and the old alike, or should I discriminate on the basis of age. Should I grant pardons to those who have recanted. Or should I punish him even though he has ceased to be a Christian, because of his past association with this name, or are only specific offenses to be punished.

Currently, in cases brought before me of those who have been accused of being Christians, I have observed the following procedures: First, I interrogated them to find out whether or not they were **Christians; those who confessed, I threatened to punish, as they endured a second and a third interrogation, after which; those who would not recant, I ordered executed.** For there is no doubt in my mind, that regardless of the nature of their gospel, stubbornness and firm defiance surely deserve punishment. There were others who held the same nonsense; but because they were Roman citizens, I commanded that they should be transported to Rome." [Note: this statement confirms Rome's great respect offered to its citizens such as found in the case of the apostle Paul in Acts 22:27-29.]

"As normally happens, because of the investigations, many accusations began to spread and many ordeals took place. On one such occasion, an anonymous record was put on public display which contained the names of many people. Of them, those who denied that they were Christians or had been one previously, when they offered up praise to our gods in the words I dictated, and with prayers brought incense and wine before a statue of your image, which I had ordered setup for this reason with the statues of the gods, and they also cursed Christ, **none of these things, it is said, those who are true Christians can be forced to do,** these I allowed to go free. Others on the informant's list admitted that they were Christians, but then denied it, saying that three years ago they stopped being one, others said they stopped many years earlier, some as long as twenty-five years ago. They all bowed down to your image and the statues of our gods, and cursed Christ.

They all believed that the only thing that they had done wrong in the past was **to meet on a weekly appointed day before sunrise and to sing hymns to Christ as to a god, and pledged not to commit crimes, but rather to refrain from committing fraud, theft, adultery, false reports, and to keep their word when called upon to do so. Afterwards, it was their tradition to depart and to gather later on in order to eat food, but**

ordinary and innocent food. Even these actions, they said, they no longer carried on after my edict in which, by your instructions, I disallowed all political gatherings. In order to find out the truth about this movement, I decided to torture two female slaves who were called deaconesses. But all I discovered was that they blindly followed a superstition.

I therefore decided to halt the investigations and to await your instructions. Because of the great number of people involved, I thought it best to seek your advice. For all members of our society will be affected regardless of their age, rank, or gender. For this superstition has spread like pestilence into our cities, villages and farms. But it does seem possible to me that it can be stopped and even cured. It is also evident that the once deserted temples have now begun to be visited once again, and that the religious ceremonies which in the past were forgotten, are now starting up again. Sacrificial animals are being brought from many districts, where previously there was no need for them. Therefore, I can envision a time when the multitudes will be reformed, if only they are given an opportunity to do so."

Trajan's reply to Pliny:

"My dear Pliny, You have followed the proper guidelines in examining the cases of those who had been accused to you as Christians. For it is not possible to lay down any general rules to serve as a kind of fixed standard on this issue. They are not to be sought out; but if they are found out and proven guilty, they are to be condemned, with the following exception, that whoever denies that he is a Christian and really proves it, by worshiping our gods, no matter what his past involvement, he should be granted a pardon. And accusations that have been posted by anonymous sources should not be used as evidence in any proceedings against them. For this would not be in keeping with the spirit of our age and would set a very dangerous example for others to follow."

Another account of Christian persecution of the early church comes from Suetonius. He was an early historian who served as a court official under the Roman Emperor Hadrian. In his work entitled the lives of the Caesars he wrote the following: **"Nero inflicted persecution on the Christians"**

A Roman Citizen's greatest statements regarding Persecution:

"Who shall separate us from the love of Christ? Shall tribulation, or distress, or persecution, or famine, or nakedness, or peril, or sword? As it is written: "For Your sake we are killed all day long; We are accounted as sheep for the slaughter." Yet in all these things we are more than conquerors through Him who loved us. For I am persuaded that neither death nor life, nor angels nor principalities nor powers, nor things present nor things to come, nor height nor depth, nor any other created thing, shall be able to separate us from the love of God which is in Christ Jesus our Lord. (Romans 8:35-39)

"And others were tortured, not accepting deliverance, that they might obtain a better resurrection. Still others had trial of mockings and scourgings, yes, and of chains and imprisonment. They were stoned, they were sawn in two, were tempted, were slain with the sword. They wandered about in sheepskins and goatskins, being destitute, afflicted, tormented; of whom the world was not worthy . . . And all these, having obtained a good testimony through faith, did not receive the promise, God having provided something better for us, that they should not be made perfect apart from us.

Hebrews 11:35-40

ACTS 21- THE EGYPTIAN

During the apostle Paul's visit to Jerusalem, Paul had an encounter with a Roman tribune who mistakenly suspects that he is the Egyptian prophet who had recently led many of the Jews into rebellion. We read in the Book of Acts 21 verses 33-38: "Then the commander came near and took him, and commanded him to be bound with two chains; and he asked him what he had done . . .

"Then as Paul was about to be led into the barracks, he said to the commander, "May I speak to you?" The commander replied, "Can you speak Greek? **Are you not the Egyptian who some time ago stirred up rebellion and led the four thousand assassins out into the wilderness?**"

Amazingly, a mention of this revolt led by a self proclaimed prophet from Egypt is confirmed in the annals of history.

The Jewish historian Josephus writing in the first century gives us this account:

"These deeds of the robbers filled the city with all sorts of impiety. And now conjurers and **deceivers persuaded the multitude to follow them into the wilderness**, and pretended that they would show them manifest wonders and signs that would be performed by the providence of God. And those that were deceived suffered the pain of their folly, for Felix brought them back and punished them. At this time **there came out of Egypt to Jerusalem a man who said he was a prophet, and advised the multitude of the common people to go along with him** to the mountain called the Mount of Olives, which lay a distance of five furlongs from the city. He said that he would show them that at his command the walls of Jerusalem would fall down, through which he promised that he would procure for them an entrance into the city. Now when Felix was informed of this he ordered his soldiers to take up their weapons, and with a great number of horsemen and footmen from Jerusalem he attacked the Egyptian and the people that were with him. He slew four hundred of them and took two hundred alive. **But the Egyptian himself escaped** from the fight and did not appear any more. And again the robbers stirred up the people to make war with the Romans."

Antiquities 20.8.5-6 (War 2.13.5-6)

Back in Acts 21, after the commander realizes that Paul is not this Egyptian rebel he sends Paul to the Roman procurator Felix for judgement. The Bible records the following:

And he called for two centurions, saying, "Prepare two hundred soldiers, seventy horsemen, and two hundred spearmen to go to Caesarea at the third hour of the night; " and provide mounts to set Paul on, and bring him safely to Felix the governor."

. . . And he (Felix) commanded him to be kept in Herod's Praetorium.

Now after five days Ananias the high priest came down with the elders and a certain orator named Tertullus. These gave evidence to the governor against Paul . . . Then Paul, after the governor had nodded to him to speak, answered: . . .

"But this I confess to you, that according to the Way which they call a sect, so I worship the God of my fathers, believing all things which are written in the Law and in the Prophets. "I have hope in God, which they themselves also accept, that there will be a resurrection of the dead, both of the just and the unjust . . . "unless it is for this one statement which I cried out, standing among them, 'Concerning the resurrection of the dead I am being judged by you this day." . . .

And after some days, when **Felix came with his wife Drusilla**, who was Jewish, he sent for Paul and heard him concerning the faith in Christ.

Now as he reasoned about righteousness, self-control, and the judgment to come, Felix was afraid and answered, "Go away for now; when I have a convenient time I will call for you." . . .
But after two years Porcius Festus succeeded Felix; and Felix, wanting to do the Jews a favor, left Paul bound. Acts 23:23-24:27

Not only is the Egyptian confirmed in history but the whole sequence of events and people that surround the apostle Paul's trials and imprisonment from Acts 21-24 are confirmed as well as recorded by Josephus:
"Claudius now sent **Felix, brother of Pallas, to take charge of Judea** . . . **Felix fell in love with Agrippa's sister, Drusilla**, who surpassed all other woman in beauty. He sent a Jewish magician named Atomus to lure her away from her husband and into Felix's arms . . . In Judea, where matters were going from bad to worse, **Felix had to capture imposters and rebels on a daily basis** . . . **When Porcius Festus replaced Felix**, the Jewish leaders accused Felix before Nero."
'Jewish Antiquities'

These statements confirm the Biblical account that Felix was indeed the procurator of Judea, that he was replaced by Porcius Festus and that Felix was married to Drusilla by adultery. And as an adulterer it would come as no surprise that Felix became afraid and convicted when Paul preached to him about righteousness, self-control, and the judgment to come.
You see the Gospel convicts us of our sins.

JESUS GREATEST WORDS ABOUT CONVICTION

"But now I go away to Him who sent Me, and none of you asks Me, 'Where are You going?' But because I have said these things to you, sorrow has filled your heart. Nevertheless I tell you the truth. It is to your advantage that I go away; for if I do not go away, the Helper will not come to you; but if I depart, I will send Him to you. **And when He has come, He will convict the world of sin, and of righteousness, and of judgment:**

"Of sin because they do not believe in me. Of righteousness, because I go to My Father and you see Me no more; of judgment, because the ruler of this world is judged."

"I still have many things to say to you, but you cannot bear them now. However, when **He, the Spirit of truth, has come, He will guide you into all truth**; for He will not speak on His own authority, but whatever He hears He will speak; and He will tell you things to come. "He will glorify Me, for He will take of what is Mine and declare it to you. All things that the Father has are Mine. Therefore I said that He will take of Mine and declare it to you."

"A little while, and you will not see Me; and again in a little while, and you will see Me, because I go to the Father." John 16:5-15 (NKJV)

THE WALL SEPARATING JEWS AND GENTILES

During excavations of Jerusalem in 1871, two archaeologists, Clermont and Ganneau, discovered what is known as the Soreg Inscription. Written in Greek, the sign warns non-Jews to keep out of the temple area. It states: **"No foreigner is to enter the barriers surrounding the sanctuary. He who is caught will have himself to blame for his death which will follow."**

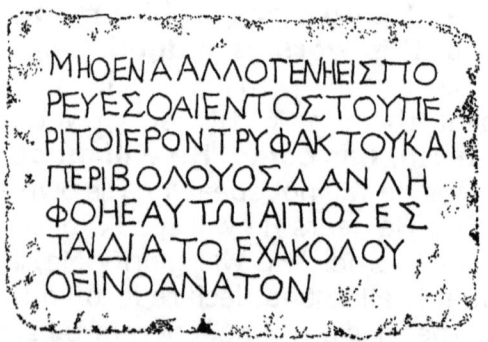

Temple Warning Inscription

The historian Josephus also mentions this inscription in chapter 15 of his work, Antiquities of the Jews:

"The center of the structure was the tallest, with the front wall being built with beams which sat upon interlocking pillars. Highly glossed stones made up this wall, so finely polished that those who looked upon it for the first time marveled at it in amazement. This was the description of the first structure. Located within it, and nearby, were steps which led up to the second structure, which was surrounded by a **stone wall used as a barrier, engraved with an inscription not allowing foreigners to enter into it under the penalty of death.**"

And it is of this inscription which the apostle Paul refers to in his letter to the Ephesians:

"Therefore remember that you, once Gentiles . . . that at that time you were without Christ, being aliens from the commonwealth of Israel and strangers from the covenants of promise, having no hope and without God in the world. But now in Christ Jesus you who once were far off have been brought near by the blood of Christ. For He Himself is our peace, who has made both one, **and has broken down the middle wall of separation** . . . that He might reconcile them both to God in one body through the cross . . . And He came and preached peace to you who were afar off and to those who were near. For through Him we both have access by one Spirit to the Father.

Now, therefore, **you are no longer strangers and foreigners**, but fellow citizens with the saints and members of the household of God, having been built on the foundation of the apostles and prophets, Jesus Christ Himself being the chief corner stone, in whom the whole building, being joined together, grows into a holy temple in the Lord, in whom you also are being built together for a dwelling place of God in the Spirit."

Ephesians 2:11-22

Old Testament   Chapter 11

ADAM, THE FLOOD & THE TOWER OF BABEL

Turning just a few pages into the Bible, to Genesis chapter 10, we read about the first cities known to man after the global flood of Noah's day. One of Noah's descendants was a man by the name of Nimrod whose kingdom included the cities of **Babel, Erech, Akkad, and Calneh** in the land of **Shinar**. Another descendant was **Asshur**, and he went forth and built **Nineveh, Rehoboth Ir, Calah, and Resen** in the land of Assyria.

These first cities lay in a land modern historians call ancient Mesopotamia which means "the land between two rivers." Those rivers being the Tigris and the Euphrates. This land would later be the staging ground for two of the world's most feared Empires, that of Assyria and Babylon. That same land which we call present day Iraq.

I remember during my college days taking a class in Western Civilization, and the very first cultures mentioned in the history book we were assigned was that of the ancient Akkadians and Sumerians who lived in Mesopotamia. And it should come as no surprise because the city state of Akkad, as well as the cities of Sumer, were mentioned in Genesis 10:10-12 long ago.

One of the most amazing finds uncovered in **Akkad** was that of a seal which possibly shows that the Akkadians knew of the story of the temptation of Adam and Eve in the Garden of Eden. George Smith of the British Museum, who lived during the middle 1800's, wrote: "One striking and important specimen of early type in the British Museum has two figures sitting one on each side of a tree, holding out their hands to the fruit, while at the back of one (the woman) is stretched a serpent.

We know well that in these early sculptures none of these figures were chance devices, but all represented events or supposed events, and figures . . . thus it is evident that a form of the story of the Fall, similar to that of Genesis, was known from early times in Babylonia."

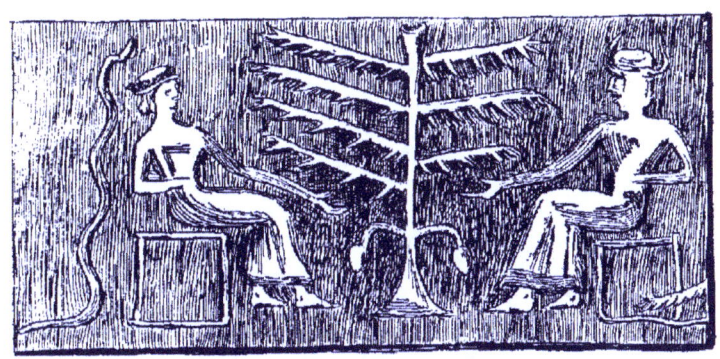

Akkadian "Temptation Seal"
From 2,300-2,200 B.C.

The first city mentioned in the Bible as being among the cities of Nimrod is **Babel**. And in fact the city's name, as well as the Tower of Babel account, is recorded outside of the Bible.

Fragments of an Assyrian tablet were discovered at Nineveh by Austen Henry Layard during the middle of the 19th century that closely parallel the Biblical Tower of Babel account. The artifacts now reside in the British Museum (registration number K.3657) and reads as follows: "his heart was evil against the father of all the gods . . . Babylon was brought into subjection, small and great alike. **He confounded their speech . . . their strong palace (tower) all the days they built**; to their strong place in the night He completely made an end . . . In His anger His word was poured out . . . **to scatter aboard He set his face, He gave this command, and their counsel was confused** . . . He saw them and the earth . . . of stopping not . . .

Bitterly they wept at **Babi(l)**."

Babel Artifact - British Museum K.3657

Sumer's oldest and most important capital city was Uruk (Biblical **Erech**). Present day Iraq possibly derived its name from this ancient city. **Uruk** is recorded on an artifact known as the 'Sumerian Kings List' which also mentions the **Elamites**. The very same Elamites who descended from **Elam**, the son of Shem, the son of Noah, as listed in Genesis 10:22.

Sumer's capital was later moved from **Erech** to **UR**. The same city which Abraham later left to go to the land of Canaan. The Bible calls this city **"Ur of the Chaldeans"** in Genesis 11:31. An inscription from Argistis, found near the city of Van, verifies this title. It states, "This is the spoil of the cities I obtained for the people of the **Khaldis** (Chaldeans) in one year."

One fascinating archeological find at Ur is that of a temple tower which the Akkadians called a ziggurat. This tower was later rebuilt by king Nabonidus of Babylon who reigned between 555 and 539 B.C.

On inscriptions found at this ziggurat, Nabonidus states that he had rebuilt the structure which he learned was originally constructed by two kings who lived 1,500 years earlier then his time. One inscription also bears the name of another Biblical Babylonian prince by the name of **Belshazzar**, who would live to see God's handwriting on the walls of Babylon as recorded in Daniel chapter 5.

Ziggurat ruins at Ur

    This ziggurat, which resembled a four sided stepped pyramid, was probably similar to that of the Biblical tower built at **Babel**. Other towers in Mesopotamia such as the one at **Ur** have been found at **Calah** (Nimrud), **Assur**, **Akkad** (Sippar), **Uruk, Cush** (Kish), Borsippa, Aqarquf, Khorabad, and Eridu, a city near Ur.

    Inscriptions from various Babylonian kings also record the construction of these temple towers which they say reached to the sky. The inscriptions use similar wording to that found in the Bible's tower of Babel account.

Hammurabi, who ruled nearly 2,000 years before Christ, states: "He restored the temple Emeteursag . . . and built the **temple tower . . . whose top is sky high."**

Much later in the sixth century B.C. Nebuchadnezzar king of Babylon wrote: "I raised the summit of the Tower of stages at Etemenanki so that **its top rivaled the heavens**."

We also know from Babylonian inscriptions that these towers reached heights of up to 300 feet.

Archaeology in this region has also uncovered one of the earliest accounts of the flood. It is listed on an artifact known as the "Sumerian Kings List" dating back to around 2,200 B.C. The inscription reads: **"The flood swept over (the earth). After the flood had swept over (the earth) (and) when the kingship was lowered (again) from heaven, kingship was (first) at Kish (Cush)."**

What is interesting about this statement is not only that the flood is mentioned, but also a city founded by **Cush**, who was the son of Ham, the son of Noah. The Bible in Genesis 10:8 states that Nimrod descended from Cush. The city of Kish (Cush) was located in the area very close to Babylon.

Another artifact from the Sumerians was found at Nippur (Biblical **Calneh**) which states: **"A flood came over the cities to destroy the seed of all mankind . . . all the wind-storms, exceedingly powerful attacked as one, At the same time, the flood swept over the culture centers. For seven days and seven nights, the flood had swept over the land. The huge boat had been tossed about by the windstorms on the great waters."**

Another fascinating artifact was found at

Nineveh, one of the cities of **Asshur** mentioned in Genesis 10:11. It gives an account of the flood somewhat similar to the Bible's account, showing they also had a knowledge of the great flood of Noah's day:

". . . build a ship, seek thou life . . . aboard the ship take thou the seed of all living things . . . All my family and kin I brought aboard the ship. The beasts of the field, the wild creatures of the field . . . I brought aboard . . ."Board thou ship and batten up thy entrance!" That stated time had arrived: He who orders unease at night, showers down a rain of blight. I watched the appearance of the weather. The weather was awesome to behold. I boarded the ship and battened up the entrance. With the first glow of dawn, a black cloud rose up from the horizon . . . Consternation over Adad reaches the heavens, Who turned to darkness all that had been light . . . For one day the south storm gathered speed as it blew, overtaking the [people] like a battle. No one could see one another . . . For six days and six nights the flood winds blew, as the south-storm swept over the land . . . On the seventh day the flood subsided . . . the flood ceased. I looked at the weather; stillness had set in. All of mankind had returned to clay . . . On mount Nisir the ship came to a halt . . . When the seventh day arrived, I set forth a dove. The dove went back and forth, but came back; since no resting place for it was visible. Then I sent forth a swallow. The swallow went forth, but came back; since no resting place for it was visible. Then I sent forth and set free a raven. The raven went forth, and seeing the waters diminished, he eats, circles, caws and turns not around. Then I let out (all) to the four winds and offered a sacrifice. I poured out a libation on the top of the mountains."

Tablet number 11 of the Gilgamesh Epic dated to the 7th century B.C. found at Nineveh gives an account of a flood with some similarities to that of the Bible.

Another of Nimrod's cities was **Calneh**, which according to the Talmud is associated with the site of Nippur.

According to Genesis 11:1-9, Nimrod's cities, which included the region of Babel, Erech, Akkad, and Calneh, were known as the land of **Shinar**.

The name **Shinar** is found in Egyptian records from Pharaoh Amenhotep II who wrote: "Now when the prince of the land of Naharin, the Prince of Hatti, and the prince of **Shinar** heard of my great victory, . . . they asked me to spare their lives."

To the Northwest of Shinar lies the cities founded by **Asshur**, who was a descendant of Noah's son Shem. His first city was named after himself, **Assur**. And just like the ruins from Akkad and Sumer, a ziggurat has also been uncovered at Assur.

Another one of his cities mentioned in Genesis 10:11 is **Calah**. The existence of this city has been found on a Royal Inscription from Assurnasirpal II, an early king of Assyria, who states "I took over again the city of **Calah**."

The Biblical city of **Resen** mentioned in Genesis 10:12 is believed to be the city of Larsia, for in Hebrew, Resen means "fortified place." The historian Xenophon recorded that Larissa was a great fortress located between the cities of Nineveh and Calneh.

The city of **Rehoboth Ir** is associated today with the Assyrian city of Khorsabad.

And of course last but not least, the great city of **Nineveh** which later became the capital of the Assyrian empire.

THE GREATEST WORDS SPOKEN ABOUT THE TEMPTATION IN THE GARDEN OF EDEN:

For since by man came death, by Man also came the resurrection of the dead. For as in Adam all die, even so in Christ all shall be made alive.
1 Corinthians 15:21-22

THE GREATEST WORDS SPOKEN ABOUT THE FLOOD:

"When once the Divine longsuffering waited in the days of Noah, while the ark was being prepared, in which a few, that is, eight souls, were saved through water.

There is also an antitype which now saves us; baptism (not the removal of the filth of the flesh, but the answer of a good conscience toward God), through the resurrection of Jesus Christ, who has gone into heaven and is at the right hand of God, angels and authorities and powers having been made subject to Him. "Therefore, since Christ suffered for us in the flesh, arm yourselves also with the same mind, for he who has suffered in the flesh has ceased from sin, that he no longer should live the rest of his time in the flesh for the lusts of men, but for the will of God. For we have spent enough of our past lifetime in doing the will of the Gentiles; when we walked in lewdness, lusts, drunkenness, revelries, drinking parties, and abominable idolatries. 1 Peter 3:20-4:3

Old Testament   Chapter 12

THE ROCK CITY

In the classic movie 'Indiana Jones and the Last Crusade', the actor Sean Connery, the original James Bond, plays Indie's elderly father whose lifetime obsession is to find the Holy Grail. Their quest to find the sacred relic leads them to the ruins of a lost city which had had been conquered by the crusaders and knights way back during medieval times. In order to find the city, the two have to travel by horseback through a winding narrow passageway. This crevice, with towering granite walls skyrocketing upwards on both sides of the canyon, finally opens up onto a spectacular view of a city, with its walls and pillars literally carved into the face of the massive rock cliffs that surround the area.

This city, which many viewers of the movie are probably unaware of, is the rock fortress of Petra, a major city of the Biblical Edomites. And although in reality the Holy Grail has never been found, the city of Petra remains as one of the greatest discoveries in the annals of Biblical archaeology. Not just because of its finding, but because of the prophecy it fulfills and the prophecy that is yet to be fulfilled in the original capital of Edom, Bozrah.

Many of the Old Testament prophets spoke out against this once mighty city that was the pride of the nation of Edom. The Edomites were the descendants of Jacob's brother Esau, as mentioned in Genesis 36:43, and they lived in the mountainous regions south of the Dead Sea.

According to the Bible, Esau's hand was always against his brother. He even plotted once to kill Jacob because he had deceived his father Isaac into giving him a blessing. And later when the children of Israel were seeking safe passage on their way to the promised land, Esau's descendants refused to allow Israel permission to travel through their territory.

Because of their constant hostility against Israel, God declared their fate in Malachi 1:2-4: "I have loved you," says the LORD. "Yet you say, 'In what way have You loved us?' Was not Esau Jacob's brother?" Says the LORD.

"Yet Jacob I have loved; But Esau I have

hated, And laid waste his mountains and his heritage For the jackals of the wilderness."

Even though Edom has said, "We have been impoverished, But we will return and build the desolate places," Thus says the LORD of hosts: "They may build, but I will throw down; They shall be called the Territory of Wickedness, And the people against whom the LORD will have indignation forever."

Did the Lord lay waste this Edomite stronghold and give it to the jackals? Oh yes. You see from 550 B.C. to 400 B.C. the Edomites were overrun by Nabatean Arabs who ransacked their territory. And although Petra was inhabited by others up until the time the Crusaders conquered it, afterwards the city was completely deserted to the jackals until being rediscovered by archaeologists in the late 1800's.

Once a mighty fortress situated on a major trade route between North Africa and Europe. Now all that is left are a bunch of empty stones, a wasteland of thorns and thistles, crawling with snakes, lizards, and owls by night, while birds of prey can be seen circling the sky's overhead by day.

During our time, the only men who come to its gates are tourist who marvel at how such a mighty kingdom could have fallen. Yet the Lord has spoken these words of judgement against Edom's cities many years in the past:

". . . the owl and the raven shall dwell in it. And He shall stretch out over it. The line of confusion and the stones of emptiness. They shall call its nobles to the kingdom, But none shall be there, and all its princes shall be nothing. And thorns shall come up in its palaces, Nettles and brambles in its fortresses; It shall be a habitation of jackals, A courtyard for ostriches. The wild beasts of the desert shall also meet with the jackals, And the wild goat shall bleat to its companion; Also the night creatures shall rest there, And find for herself a place of rest. There the arrow snake shall make her nest and lay eggs And hatch, and gather them under her shadow; There also shall the hawks be gathered, Every one with her mate. "Search from the book of the LORD, and read: Not one of these shall fail; Not one shall lack her mate. For My mouth has commanded it, and His Spirit has gathered them."

Isaiah 34:11-16

God said that he would strip this rock fortress free of all the Edomites and make their empty stones a marvel for all that pass by:

"For I have sworn by Myself," says the LORD, "that Bozrah shall become a desolation, a reproach, a waste, and a curse. And all its cities shall be perpetual wastes." I have heard a message from the LORD, And an ambassador has been sent to the nations: "Gather together, come against her, And rise up to battle! "For indeed, I will make you small among nations, Despised among men. Your fierceness has deceived you, The pride of your heart, O you who dwell in the clefts of the rock, Who hold the height of the hill! Though you make your nest as high as the eagle, I will bring you down from there," says the LORD. "Edom also shall be an astonishment; Everyone who goes by it will be astonished And will hiss at all its plagues. As in the overthrow of Sodom and Gomorrah and their neighbors," says the LORD, "No one shall remain there, Nor shall a son of man dwell in it."

Jeremiah 49:13-18

In Ezekiel 25:14, God mentions that the nation of Israel would one day take out the Lord's vengeance on Edom, and history confirms that this prophecy has been fulfilled.

The first century Jewish historian Josephus gives us one account of Israel's defeat of Edom:

"The Idumeans (formerly the Edomites) surrendered to Hycranus who allowed them to live as long as they agreed to circumcise their sons and to

abide by Jewish customs. This they did, and from that point on they followed the practices of the Jews."
(Antiquities Book 13 Chap 9:1)

Another account can be found in the historical texts of the book of Maccabees:
"At the same time the Idumeans, who held some important strongholds, were harassing the Jews; . . . Maccabeus and his companions, after public prayers asking God to be their ally, moved quickly against the strongholds of the Idumeans (the Edomites). Attacking vigorously, they gained control of the places, drove back all who manned the walls, and cut down those who opposed them, killing as many as twenty thousand men."
(2 Maccabees 10:15-17)

The Lord's vengeance against the Edomites was complete, and to this very day the mountains of Seir, Bozrah, Teman and Petra all lie as a barren wasteland in fulfillment of Scripture.

But there is still one prophecy given by the Lord about one of Edom's cities, Bozrah, that is still yet to come. It will be fulfilled when Christ returns to this earth in all power and great glory.

Isaiah 62:11-63:8 says: "Indeed the LORD has proclaimed To the end of the world: "Say to the daughter of Zion, 'Surely your salvation is coming; Behold, His reward is with Him, And His work before Him.' "And they shall call them The Holy People, The Redeemed of the LORD; And you shall be called Sought Out, A City Not Forsaken.

Who is this who comes from Edom, With dyed garments from Bozrah, This One who is glorious in His apparel, Traveling in the greatness of His strength?; "I who speak in righteousness, mighty to save." Why is Your apparel red, And Your garments like one who treads in the winepress? "I have trodden the winepress alone, And from the peoples no one was with Me. For I have trodden them in My anger,

And trampled them in My fury; Their blood is sprinkled upon My garments, And I have stained all My robes. For the day of vengeance is in My heart, And the year of My redeemed has come. I looked, but there was no one to help, And I wondered That there was no one to uphold; Therefore My own arm brought salvation for Me; And My own fury, it sustained Me. I have trodden down the peoples in My anger, Made them drunk in My fury, And brought down their strength to the earth." I will mention the lovingkindnesses of the LORD And the praises of the LORD, According to all that the LORD has bestowed on us, And the great goodness toward the house of Israel, Which He has bestowed on them according to His mercies, According to the multitude of His lovingkindnesses. For He said, "Surely they are My people, Children who will not lie." So He became their Savior."

THE GREATEST PROPHECY CONCERNING PETRA:

Upon this Rock (Petra) I will build my church, and the gates of hell shall not prevail against it. (The Petra in this passage refers to Jesus Christ, the Lord himself. For a mighty rock fortress is our God.)

THE GREATEST SONG TO BE SUNG ABOUT A MIGHTY ROCK FORTRESS:

> A mighty fortress is our God,
> A stronghold never failing;
> Our helper He amid the flood
> Of mortal ills prevailing;
> For still our ancient foe
> Does seek to work us woe;
> His craft and power are great,
> And armed with cruel hate,
> On earth is not His equal

Did we in our own strength confide,
Our striving would be losing;
Were not the right Man on our side,
The Man of God's own choosing;
Do you ask who that may be?
Christ Jesus, it is He;
Lord Sabboth is His name,
From age to age the same,
And He must win the battle.

And though this world, with devils filled,
Should threaten to undo us,
We will not fear, for God hath willed
His truth to triumph through us;
The prince of Darkness grim,
We tremble not for him;
His rage we can endure,
For lo, his doom is sure,
One little word shall fell him.

That word above all earthly powers,
No thanks to them, abideth;
The Spirit and the gifts are ours
Through Him who with us sideth:
Let goods and kindred go,
This mortal life also;
The body they may kill:
God's truth abideth still,
His kingdom is forever.

LOT'S DESCENDANTS

After Lot fled the city of Sodom, which God destroyed with fire and brimstone because of their sins of homosexuality, he had a son named Ben-Ammi. According to Genesis 19:38 he was the father of the Ammonites.

The Ammonites became one of Israel's most hated enemies. They were one of the nations that hired Balaam to curse Israel at the time of Moses, as recorded in Nehemiah 13:1-2. Because of that action, God declared in Deuteronomy 23:3 that no Ammonite could ever enter into the assembly of the Lord.

Biblical archaeology has brought to light many artifacts from the kings of Ammon. One such seal was found stamped with the words: **"Milqom, the steward of Baalis."**

Baalis is mentioned in the Bible as being the king who had Gedaliah the governor of Judah assassinated, as recorded in Jeremiah 40:13-14:

"Moreover Johanan the son of Kareah and all the captains of the forces that were in the fields came to **Gedaliah** at Mizpah, and said to him, "Do you certainly know that **Baalis the king of the Ammonites** has sent Ishmael the son of Nethaniah to murder you?" But **Gedaliah** the son of Ahikam did not believe them."

Gedaliah's seal has also been unearthed in archaeology.

Gedaliah Seal

A mention of the Ammonite's was also found on a bronze bottle near Amman Jordan. The relic belonged to Amminadab the first, the king of the Ammonites who lived around 650 B.C. It is engraved with the words: **"The Sons of Ammon."**

Another famous artifact known as the monolith inscription, from Shalmaneser the third, mentions the leader of an Ammonite army along with Ahab the king of Israel. The inscription reads:

"To strengthen his forces he was assisted by Hadadzer of Damascus who had 1,200 chariots and cavalrymen, along with 20,000 soldiers on foot . . . 2,000 chariots and 10,000 troops of **Ahab from Israel . . . military forces of Basa, the son of Ruhubi, the Ammonite.** Combined they numbered twelve kings."

Inscription mentioning Ahab of Israel and the king of Ammon.

Do not follow the example of the Ammonites. But flee temptation like their ancestor Lot.

"For if God did not spare the angels who sinned, but cast them down to hell and delivered them into chains of darkness, to be reserved for judgment; and did not spare the ancient world, but saved Noah, one of eight people, a preacher of righteousness, bringing in the flood on the world of the ungodly; and turning the cities of Sodom and Gomorrah into ashes, condemned them to destruction, making them an example to those who afterward would live ungodly; and **delivered righteous Lot**, who was oppressed by the filthy conduct of the wicked **(for that righteous man, dwelling among them, tormented his righteous soul from day to day by seeing and hearing their lawless deeds); then the Lord knows how to deliver the godly out of temptations** and to reserve the unjust under punishment for the day of judgment."

2 Peter 2:4-9

JEHU AND HAZAEL

Ancient Assyrian records from the time of Shalmaneser III verify events and kings mentioned in the Bible during the time of the prophets Elijah and Elisha.

The first Assyrian record mentions how Hazael, the king of Syria, seized the throne from Hadadezer. The ancient text reads: "I was victorious over Hadadezer of Damascus along with his allies which numbered twelve kings. His warriors, numbering 20,900, laid slain upon the ground, while his remaining army was forced to withdraw to the Orontes river. There they retreated in order to spare their lives. **Afterwards, Hadadezer died and Hazael, the son of a worthless man, seized the throne.** He formed a large army and waged war against me. I engaged him in battle and claimed the victory. He retreated in order to save his life." (Ancient Near Eastern Texts 280)

This record verifies the Biblical account of Hazael seizing the throne from Hadadezer as mentioned in 2 Kings 8:7-15: "Then Elisha went to Damascus, and Ben-Hadad (Hadadezer) king of Syria was sick; and it was told him, saying, "The man of God has come here." And the king said to Hazael, "Take a present in your hand, and go to meet the man of God, and inquire of the LORD by him, saying, 'Shall I recover from this disease?' "So Hazael went to meet him and took a present with him, of every good thing of Damascus, forty camel-loads; and he came and stood before him, and said, "Your son Ben-Hadad king of Syria has sent me to you, saying, 'Shall I recover from this disease?' "

And Elisha said to him, "Go, say to him, 'You shall certainly recover.' However the LORD has shown me that he will really die." Then he set his countenance in a stare until he was ashamed; and the man of God wept. And Hazael said, "Why is my lord weeping?" He answered, "Because I know the evil that you will do to the children of Israel: Their strongholds you will set on fire, and their young men you will kill with the sword; and you will dash their children, and rip open their women with child." So Hazael said, "But what is your servant; a dog, that he should do this gross thing?" And Elisha answered, "The LORD has shown me that you will become king over Syria." Then he departed from Elisha, and came to his master, who said to him, "What did Elisha say to you?" And he answered, "He told me you would surely recover." But it happened on the next day that he took a thick cloth and dipped it in water, and spread it over his face so that he died; and **Hazael reigned in his place**."

Another inscription from Shalmaneser found on the Black Obelisk mentions the king of Israel, Jehu, who ruled during the time of Hazael. The Obelisk also shows a depiction of Jehu bowing down before the Assyrian king offering his tribute. The inscription reads: "I received tribute from Jehu, from the house of Omri; I received from him silver,

Jehu's tribute to Shalmaneser
Black Obelisk Artifact

gold, a golden bowl, a golden vase . . . and a staff for a king."

THE SERVANTS OF GOD ARE NOT ALONE

Suddenly a voice came to him, and said, "What are you doing here, Elijah?" And he said, "I have been very zealous for the LORD God of hosts; because the children of Israel have forsaken Your covenant, torn down Your altars, and killed Your prophets with the sword. **I alone am left; and they seek to take my life.**"

Then the LORD said to him: "Go, return on your way to the Wilderness of Damascus; and when you arrive, **anoint Hazael as king over Syria. Also you shall anoint Jehu the son of Nimshi as king over Israel.** And Elisha the son of Shaphat of Abel Meholah you shall anoint as prophet in your place."

"It shall be that whoever escapes the sword of Hazael, Jehu will kill, and whoever escapes the sword of Jehu, Elisha will kill. **Yet I have reserved seven thousand in Israel, all whose knees have not bowed to Baal, and every mouth that has not kissed him.**" 1 Kings 19:13-18

And Jesus came and spoke to them, saying, "All authority has been given to Me in heaven and on earth. "Go therefore and make disciples of all the nations, baptizing them in the name of the Father and of the Son and of the Holy Spirit, "teaching them to observe all things that I have commanded you; and lo, **I am with you always, even to the end of the age.**" Amen.

Matthew 28:18-20

KING UZZIAH

Uzziah Burial Inscription

In a Russian Orthodox monastery located on the Mount of Olives, an inscription was discovered bearing the name of King Uzziah. The inscription reads: **"To this place, the remains of Uzziah, King of Judah, were placed. Do not disturb"**

There are other inscriptions from the Assyrian king Tiglath-Pileser III, which scholars argue over, which may mention him as well. One translation made from one of the artifacts states:
"During my campaigns, I received tribute of Azariah (Uzziah) of Judah [Azri(au) of Iuda]"
ANET 282

Uzziah and the story that led to his downfall is mentioned in 2Chronicles 26:
"Uzziah was sixteen years old when he became king, and he reigned fifty-two years in Jerusalem . . . He sought God in the days of Zechariah, who had understanding in the visions of God; and as long as he sought the LORD, God made him prosper . . .

And he made devices in Jerusalem, invented by skillful men, to be on the towers and the corners, to shoot arrows and large stones. So his fame spread far and wide, for he was marvelously helped till he became strong.

But when he was strong his heart was lifted up, to his destruction, for he transgressed against the LORD his God by entering the temple of the LORD to burn incense on the altar of incense. So Azariah the priest went in after him, and with him were eighty priests of the LORD; valiant men. And they withstood King Uzziah, and said to him, "It is not for you, Uzziah, to burn incense to the LORD, but for the priests, the sons of Aaron, who are consecrated to burn incense. Get out of the sanctuary, for you have trespassed! You shall have no honor from the LORD God."

Then Uzziah became furious; and he had a censer in his hand to burn incense. And while he was angry with the priests, leprosy broke out on his forehead, before the priests in the house of the LORD, beside the incense altar. And Azariah the chief priest and all the priests looked at him, and there, on his forehead, he was leprous; so they thrust him out of that place. Indeed he also hurried to get out, because the LORD had struck him.

King Uzziah was a leper until the day of his death. He dwelt in an isolated house, because he was a leper; for he was cut off from the house of the LORD. Then Jotham his son was over the king's house, judging the people of the land.

Now the rest of the acts of Uzziah, from first to last, the prophet Isaiah the son of Amoz wrote. So Uzziah rested with his fathers, and they buried him with his fathers in the field of burial which belonged to the kings, for they said, "He is a leper." Then Jotham his son reigned in his place."

THE GREATEST CRY THE YEAR UZZIAH DIED:

"In the year that King Uzziah died, I saw the Lord sitting on a throne, high and lifted up, and the train of His robe filled the temple.

Above it stood seraphim; each one had six wings: with two he covered his face, with two he covered his feet, and with two he flew. And one cried to another and said: **"Holy, holy, holy is the LORD of hosts; The whole earth is full of His glory!"**

So I said: "Woe is me, for I am undone! Because I am a man of unclean lips, And I dwell in the midst of a people of unclean lips; For my eyes have seen the King, the Lord of hosts."

Isaiah 6:1-5

THIS KING, THE LORD OF HOSTS, IS JESUS CHRIST!

"Behold, I send My messenger, And he will prepare the way before Me. And the Lord, whom you seek, Will suddenly come to His temple, Even the Messenger of the covenant, In whom you delight. Behold, He is coming," Says the LORD of hosts."

Malachi 3:1

AHAZ, KING OF JUDAH

Unlike his father, King Jotham, who the Bible says: "Became mighty, and ordered his ways before the Lord," Ahaz became a wicked ruler. The Bible records in 2Kings 16:3 that he even sacrificed his own sons in the fire, not much unlike the practice of modern day abortionists who sacrifice the sons and daughters of many for mere profit.

A mention of Ahaz, found outside of the Bible, was taken from a clay building inscription of Tiglath-Pileser III. In accounts from his battles against Israel he records the following:

"From these I received tribute . . . **Ahaz, the king of Judah . . . including gold, silver,** iron, fine cloth and many garments made from wool that was dyed in purple . . . as well as all kinds of lavish gifts from many nations and from the kings that rule over them." ANET 282

This confirms 2Kings 16:8 which states:

"**And Ahaz took the silver and gold** that was found in the house of the LORD, and in the treasuries of the king's house, and sent it as a present to the king of Assyria."

The reason God sent Tiglath-Pileser III and his horde of Assyrians against Ahaz can be found in 2Chronicles 28:19-21:

"For the LORD brought Judah low because of Ahaz king of Israel, for he had encouraged moral decline in Judah and had been continually unfaithful to the LORD.

Also Tiglath-Pileser king of Assyria came to him and distressed him, and did not assist him. For Ahaz took part of the treasures from the house of the LORD, from the house of the king, and from the leaders, and he gave it to the king of Assyria; but he did not help him."

GOD'S GREATEST STATEMENT TO AHAZ:

"Moreover the LORD spoke again to Ahaz, saying, "Ask a sign for yourself from the LORD your God; ask it either in the depth or in the height above."
But Ahaz said, "I will not ask, nor will I test the LORD!"
Then he said, "Hear now, O house of David! Is it a small thing for you to weary men, but will you weary my God also?
"Therefore the Lord Himself will give you a sign: **Behold, the virgin shall conceive and bear a Son, and shall call His name Immanuel.**"

Isaiah 7:10-14

SARGON, KING OF ASSYRIA

Isaiah the prophet, in one of God's prophecies regarding a judgement against the nations of Egypt and Ethiopia, mentions an Assyrian king by the name of Sargon.

This posed a problem to archaeologists back in the earliest days of their field of study, because an obelisk stone with the names of all the Assyrian kings that had ruled that kingdom was uncovered which made no mention of Sargon. On its discovery the University of Chicago made a bold statement that they had found a glaring contradiction in the Bible. They assumed the Scripture was in error since Sargon's name wasn't found engraved on this stone.

But a funny thing occurred, you could say it was God's little joke on men of science. Eventually they found the royal palace of Sargon, and a majestic one it was at that. How come they knew it was Sargon's palace? Well, because the bricks lining the palace walls were engraved with his name.

Not only was his name found, but his capture of the city of Ashdod, as mentioned in Isaiah 20, was engraved on the palace walls as well. And not only that, but digs from the city of Ashdod itself later turned up fragments from a monument which recorded this victory.

One of the inscriptions read: **"Sargon, king of Assyria, who conquered Samaria and the entire region of Israel, he who made captives of Ashdod."** (ANET 284)

Displayed in the British museum is this monument which stood at the entrance of Sargon's palace. On this statue of a winged bull there is an inscription listing Sargon's titles and achievements.

Another Inscription reads: "In my first year I besieged and conquered Samaria . . . I lead away 27,290 prisoners . . . I ordered tribute to be made to me . . . Hanno king of Gaza and also Sib'e the tartan of Egypt set out to engage me in battle. I defeated them . . . I received tribute from (pharaoh) Piye of Egypt . . . Iamani of Ashdod fled to the frontier of Egypt which belongs to Ethiopia . . . Frightened of my power, the king of Ethiopia put chains on Iamani's hands and feet and sent him to me. I conquered **the towns of Samaria and all Israel.**" ANET 284-285

Well, It seems like archaeology always catches up to the truth found in the Bible. For the Bible states that the entire region was looking for Egypt and Ethiopia to help them fight against the Assyrian king, but instead both countries became vassals of Sargon. And a future Assyrian king, Esarhaddon, would attack both Egypt and Ethiopia and lead them away as captives so that what Isaiah the prophet had spoken came to pass.

"**In the year that Tartan came to Ashdod, when Sargon the king of Assyria sent him, and he fought against Ashdod and took it,** at the same time the LORD spoke by Isaiah the son of Amoz, saying, "Go, and remove the sackcloth from your body, and take your sandals off your feet." And he did so, walking naked and barefoot.

Then the LORD said, "Just as My servant Isaiah has walked naked and barefoot three years for a sign and a wonder against Egypt and Ethiopia, "so shall the king of Assyria lead away the Egyptians as prisoners and the Ethiopians as captives, young and old, naked and barefoot, with their buttocks uncovered, to the shame of Egypt. "Then they shall be afraid and ashamed of Ethiopia their expectation and Egypt their glory. "And the inhabitant of this territory will say in that day, 'Surely such is our expectation, wherever we flee for help to be delivered from the king of Assyria; **and how shall we escape**?' " Isaiah 20

The inhabitants of the land asked one of the most important questions a man or woman can ever ask. It is one concerning who would deliver them, "How shall we escape?"

The Bible gives us that answer.

"**He has delivered us** from the power of darkness and conveyed us into the kingdom of the Son of His love, in whom we have redemption through His blood, the forgiveness of sins."
Colossians 1:13-14

How shall we escape if we refuse so great a salvation!

MANASSEH, SON OF HEZEKIAH

An artifact has been found in the annals of archaeology that bears witness to Manasseh, who was the son of king Hezekiah.

Manasseh, who also became king of Judah, is mentioned by the Assyrian king Esarhaddon who began his reign about 680 years before Christ. The inscription lists kings who were under his submission as contributing materials to furnish his royal palace. It reads as follows:

"I commanded the kings from the region of Hatti as well as the areas on the other side of the Euphrates including Balu, king of Tyre, **Manasseh, king of Judah** . . . ; a total of 22 kings from Hatti, the seashore and islands, all of them were given the difficult task of transporting building materials to my palace in Nineveh, the city over which I am king."

Esarhaddon Prism located in the British Museum mentions "Manasseh of Judah" ANET 291

The story of King Manasseh is a story of a man who went from being one of the most vile and wicked sinners ever, to a saint. From an enemy of God, to a servant of God. A man under God's judgement, to a man under God's Grace and Mercy. His story can be found in 2 Chronicles 33:

'Manasseh was twelve years old when he became king, and he reigned fifty-five years in Jerusalem. But he did evil in the sight of the LORD, according to the abominations of the nations whom the LORD had cast out before the children of Israel. For he rebuilt the high places which Hezekiah his father had broken down; he raised up altars for the Baals, and made wooden images; and he worshiped all the host of heaven and served them. He also built altars in the house of the LORD, of which the LORD had said, "In Jerusalem shall My name be forever." And he built altars for all the host of heaven in the two courts of the house of the LORD. Also he caused his sons to pass through the fire in the Valley of the Son of Hinnom; he practiced soothsaying, used witchcraft and sorcery, and consulted mediums and spiritists. He did much evil in the sight of the LORD, to provoke Him to anger.

He even set a carved image, the idol which he had made, in the house of God, of which God had said to David and to Solomon his son, "In this house and in Jerusalem, which I have chosen out of all the tribes of Israel, I will put My name forever; "and I will not again remove the foot of Israel from the land which I have appointed for your fathers; only if they are careful to do all that I have commanded them, according to the whole law and the statutes and the ordinances by the hand of Moses." So Manasseh seduced Judah and the inhabitants of Jerusalem to do more evil than the nations whom the LORD had destroyed before the children of Israel.

And the LORD spoke to Manasseh and his people, but they would not listen. Therefore the LORD brought upon them the captains of the army of the king of Assyria, who took Manasseh with hooks, bound him with bronze fetters, and carried him off to Babylon."

(Note: The reference to Manasseh's captivity to Babylon was once commonly held by liberals as a mistake on the part of the Bible, because Nineveh was the capital of Esarhaddon's Assyrian empire.
However, inscriptions from Esarhaddon prove that he did indeed rebuild Babylon. One such inscription reads: "Esarhaddon ... king of Assyria, governor of Babylon.")

"Now when he was in affliction, he implored the LORD his God, and humbled himself greatly before the God of his fathers, and prayed to Him; and He received his entreaty, heard his supplication, and brought him back to Jerusalem into his kingdom. Then Manasseh knew that the LORD was God.

After this he built a wall outside the City of David on the west side of Gihon, in the valley, as far as the entrance of the Fish Gate; and it enclosed Ophel, and he raised it to a very great height. Then he put military captains in all the fortified cities of Judah.

He took away the foreign gods and the idol from the house of the LORD, and all the altars that he had built in the mount of the house of the LORD and in Jerusalem; and he cast them out of the city. He also repaired the altar of the LORD, sacrificed peace offerings and thank offerings on it, and commanded Judah to serve the LORD God of Israel. Nevertheless the people still sacrificed on the high places, but only to the LORD their God."

LIKE MANASSEH YOU MUST HUMBLE YOURSELF BEFORE GOD:
"God resists the proud, But gives grace to the humble." Therefore submit to God. Resist the devil and he will flee from you. Draw near to God and He will draw near to you. Cleanse your hands, you sinners; and purify your hearts, you double-minded. Lament and mourn and weep! Let your laughter be turned to mourning and your joy to gloom. Humble yourselves in the sight of the Lord, and He will lift you up." James 4:6-9

LIKE MANASSEH YOU MUST REPENT:

Repentance means to change your heart and mind towards God. To turn to him and to turn away from your sins.
Ezekiel 18:30-32: "Therefore I will judge you, O house of Israel, every one according to his ways," says the Lord GOD. "Repent, and turn from all your transgressions, so that iniquity will not be your ruin. "Cast away from you all the transgressions which you have committed, and get yourselves a new heart and a new spirit. For why should you die, O house of Israel?
"For I have no pleasure in the death of one who dies," says the Lord GOD. "Therefore turn and live!"

FAITH WITHOUT REPENTANCE IS NOT FAITH AND REPENTANCE WITHOUT FAITH IN CHRIST WILL NOT SAVE:

Acts 20:21: "repentance toward God and faith toward our Lord Jesus Christ."

Mark 1:15: "The time is fulfilled, and the kingdom of God is at hand. Repent, and believe in the gospel."

JEREMIAH'S ENEMY

Jeremiah was one of the prophets who God used to deliver a message of pending doom upon a nation which had refused to heed His commands. And when the people heard the unpleasant news, some of the leaders of Judah wanted to kill Jeremiah. One such man was named Jehucal, the son of Shelemiah, a high-ranking prince who served under King Zedekiah. Another was Gedaliah, the son of Pashhur.

Seal impressions once made by both Jehucal and Gedaliah were recently uncovered in Jerusalem, a few meters apart, and dated to shortly before the destruction of the city by the Babylonians.

The first seal reads: **"Belonging to Jehucal, son of Shelemiah, son of Shovi."**

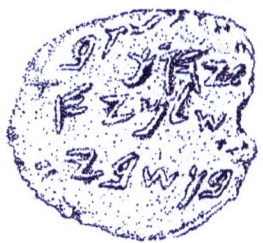

Seal of Jehucal son of Shelemiah

Seal of Gedaliah son of Pashhur

His father, Shelemiah, may also be the same man mentioned on another artifact known as Lachish letter IX which says: "May Yahweh cause my lord to hear tidings of peace! . . . Return word to my servant through **Shelemiah**, giving us instructions as to what action we shall take tomorrow!"

The second seal reads: **"Gedalyahu, son of Pashhur."**

Jeremiah's dealings with Jehucal and Gedaliah are recounted in the following passages of Scripture:

"Now King Zedekiah the son of Josiah reigned instead of Coniah the son of Jehoiakim, whom Nebuchadnezzar king of Babylon made king in the land of Judah. **But neither he nor his servants nor the people of the land gave heed to the words of the LORD which He spoke by the prophet Jeremiah.**

And Zedekiah the king sent **Jehucal the son of Shelemiah**, and Zephaniah the son of Maaseiah, the priest, to the prophet Jeremiah, saying, "Pray now to the LORD our God for us." . . . Now Shephatiah the son of Mattan, **Gedaliah the son of Pashhur**, Jehucal the son of Shelemiah, and Pashhur the son of Malchiah heard the words that Jeremiah had spoken to all the people, saying, "Thus says the LORD: 'He who remains in this city (Jerusalem) shall die by the sword, by famine, and by pestilence; `but he who goes over to the Chaldeans shall live; his life shall be as a prize to him, and he shall live.' "Thus says the LORD: 'This city shall surely be given into the hand of the king of Babylon's army, which shall take it.' "

Therefore the princes said to the king, "Please, let this man be put to death, for thus he weakens the hands of the men of war who remain in this city, and the hands of all the people, by speaking such words to them. For this man does not seek the welfare of this people, but their harm."

Then Zedekiah the king said, "Look, he is in your hand. For the king can do nothing against you."

So they took Jeremiah and cast him into the dungeon of Malchiah the king's son, which was in the court of the prison, and they let Jeremiah down with ropes. And in the dungeon there was no water, but mire. So Jeremiah sank in the mire. Now Ebed-Melech the Ethiopian, one of the eunuchs, who was in the king's house, heard that they had put Jeremiah in the dungeon. When the king was sitting at the Gate of Benjamin, Ebed-Melech went out of the king's house and spoke to the king, saying: "My lord the king, these men have done evil in all that they have done to Jeremiah the prophet, whom they have cast into the dungeon, and he is likely to die from hunger in the place where he is. For there is no more bread in the city."

Then the king commanded Ebed-Melech the Ethiopian, saying, "Take from here thirty men with you, and lift Jeremiah the prophet out of the dungeon before he dies."

Jeremiah 37:1-38:10

WANT TO BE HEARD?
GIVE HEED TO THE WORDS OF THE LORD

"Then the word of the LORD came to Zechariah, saying, "Thus says the LORD of hosts: 'Execute true justice, Show mercy and compassion Everyone to his brother. Do not oppress the widow or the fatherless, The alien or the poor. Let none of you plan evil in his heart Against his brother'

"But they refused to heed, shrugged their shoulders, and stopped their ears so that they could not hear. "Yes, **they made their hearts like flint, refusing to hear the law and the words which the LORD of hosts had sent by His Spirit through the former prophets. Thus great wrath came from the LORD of hosts.**

"Therefore it happened, that just as He proclaimed and they would not hear, so they called out and I would not listen" says the **LORD of hosts."** Zechariah 7:8-13

KING CYRUS OF PERSIA

Tomb of Cyrus the Great

Nearly one hundred and sixty years before king Cyrus was ever born, God declared to the prophet Isaiah that he would raise up this man, His shepherd, to rebuild His city, even though at the time of Isaiah, Jerusalem was prospering and wouldn't be destroyed for another 100 years by Nebuchadnezzar the king of Babylon.

The Lord's prophecy begins at Isaiah 44:28: **'Who says of Cyrus, 'He is My shepherd, And he shall perform all My pleasure, Saying to Jerusalem, "You shall be built," And to the temple, "Your foundation shall be laid." '**

The Greek historian Herodotus, in Volume 1 of his histories, records the wonderful story of how Cyrus miraculously escaped death at the time of his birth, and how he was brought up by a **shepherd** who wasn't even his father. Thus, fulfilling God's spoken word to the prophet Isaiah.

Herodotus wrote: "Astyages, the son of Cyaxares, became king. He had a fascinating dream concerning his daughter Mandane. In his dream he envisioned a stream of water flowing from her that flooded his capital as well as all of Asia. He told this vision to the Magi who had the gift of interpreting dreams, and who gave its meaning to him, whereas he became greatly terrified . . . Learning that she was now with child and her time for giving birth was near, he sent Mandane away to Persia. When she arrived there, he put a guard over her, with plans to kill the child after she gave birth (*see Isaiah 45:10-13); for when the Magi had interpreted the vision they told him that the son of his daughter would reign over Asia instead of him. To keep this from happening, immediately following the birth of Cyrus, Astyages sent for Harpagus, a man of his own house and a faithful Mede, to whom he trusted all his affairs, and addressed him saying . . . "Harpagus, take the son born of my daughter Mandane, and steal him away to your house and slay him there. Then bury him as you see fit." When Harpagus had reluctantly agreed, the child was given into his hands, wrapped in the swaddling cloth of death, and he weeping went quickly to his home . . . speaking, "My hands will not carry out his will, nor do I want any part of this murder . . . After he had said this, he sent a messenger to bring back a man named Mitradates, one of the **shepherds** . . . Coming quickly at his request, the shepherd arrived and Harpagus said to him "Astyages commands you to take this child into the wildest part of the hills, and there abandon him, that he should die a sudden death. And he told me to tell you, that if you do not kill the boy, but allow him to escape, you will be put to the death by the most painful of methods. I myself have been given orders to make sure the child dies."

At this command the herdsman took the child into his arms, and traveled back the way he had come till he reached his flocks . . . **With this the shepherd uncovered the infant**, and showed him to his wife, who, when she saw how fine and beautiful the child was, broke down into tears, and falling at her husbands knees, begged him not to kill the babe; . . . so the child, whom he was commanded to destroy, was handed over to his wife . . . "

Thus, Cyrus was raised early to be a shepherd fulfilling God's word to Isaiah.

The second part of Isaiah's prophecy states that Cyrus would **declare Jerusalem and the temple to be rebuilt**. According to the Bible, King Cyrus of Persia along with his ally, Darius the Mede, invaded the Empire of Babylon bringing its downfall.

The following is an account from King Cyrus which was found inscribed on a clay barrel known as the Cyrus Cylinder and now on display in the British Museum. He mentions how he conquered Babylon, returned exiles to their former lands, returned the articles of worship to the sacred cities and commanded that the temples where they worshiped should be rebuilt. The Inscription reads:

"The number of men in his army were so great, resembling that of water in a river, which could not be counted, marched forward, their weapons stashed away. Without engaging the enemy, he was able to enter Babylon without causing any damage to the city. Into my hands, Nabonidus was delivered, the king who did not worship him . . . **"To the sacred cities located on the other side of the Tigris river, I sent back to the ruins of their holy places, the articles which were used in their sanctuaries. I also allowed to return to their homes the former citizens of the land, . . . I also made an effort to repair their dwelling places."**

Cyrus Cylinder

The next prophecy confirmed by history is found in Isaiah 44:27: "Who says to the deep. Be dry! **And I will dry up your rivers.**'

And Isaiah 45:1-2 which says: "Thus says the LORD to His anointed, To Cyrus, whose right hand I have held; **To subdue nations before him and loose the armor of kings, To open before him the double doors, So that the gates will not be shut.** 'I will go before you and make the crooked places straight; **I will break in pieces the gates of bronze.**"

The fulfillment of these prophecies are confirmed by the historian Herodotus who wrote: "The land of Assyria possesses a great number of cities, the strongest and most well known being **Babylon**, . . . The following is a description of the place: . . . Along the edges of the top wall, they built single room structures each facing one another, leaving enough space between them to turn a four-horse chariot. **A hundred gates, all of brass, with bronze lintels and side-posts** make up the circuit of the wall . . . The city is divided into two sections by the river running through it. This river is known as the Euphrates, a wide, deep, and very swift stream, which begins in Armenia, and ends at the Erythraean sea . . . At the rivers entry points are low gates in the fence that flank the stream, which are similar in design to the **great gates in the outer wall, made of brass, and which open toward the water** . . .

Cyrus marched in the direction of Babylon and came to the banks of the Gyndes, a river which starts in the Matienian mountains and flows through the land of the Dardanians, and discharges into the Tigris river. The Tigris then continues to flow past the city of Opis, and empties into the Erythraean sea. Since the Gyndes could only be crossed by boat, Cyrus stopped at the river. One of his favorite white horses, which went along on his march, bolted off and tried to cross the river by itself, galloping into the water the horse was taken hold of by the current which swept him downstream and plunged him to his death.

Cyrus became furious with rage **and vowed to break the river's strength,** saying that future generations would be able to cross it without getting their knees wet . . . His plans to attack Babylon were now put on hold, and He divided his troops into two regiments. With the use of ropes he began to mark off areas on each side of the Gyndes, leading off from it in all directions, one hundred and eighty planned trenches per side. He then commanded his forces to dig opposite one another on both banks. His threat to break the river soon became reality with the assistance of a great a number of workers. But it came at a cost, the whole summer season was now lost.

Having defeated the river Gyndes, by diverting it into three hundred and sixty channels, Cyrus waited for next spring to march against Babylon. A short distance outside of the city wall, the Babylonians army was waiting for him. A battle then ensued, in which the Persian king defeated the Babylonians, who then withdrew into their fortress. Here they shut themselves up, and made fun of his siege, for they had prepared against his attack by storing up food within the city that would last for many years; for when they saw **Cyrus conquering nation after**

nation, they were convinced that he would never stop, and that sooner or later he would try to overpower them.

Now Cyrus did not know how to proceed, for many days had passed and he made little progress in conquering the city. Finally, either someone suggested a plan of action, or he himself came up with the idea, which he proceeded to follow. Placing a regiment of his troops at the spot where the river enters the city, and another group at the back where the river exits. He ordered them to march into the city as soon as the river became shallow enough for them to forge. He and his army then withdrew back to the place where Nitocris dug the lake for the river, proceeding to do exactly what she had done in the past; he diverted the Euphrates by a canal into the old lake bed, which was now a marsh. The river began to lower to such a level that it was now possible to cross. At this moment, the Persian army that was left behind at Babylon entered the stream, whose level reached midway up a man's thigh, and they marched into the city.

Had the Babylonians been aware of what Cyrus was up to, or had seen their danger, they could have kept the Persians from entering the city and would have destroyed his army; for they could have closed all the street-gates which overlooked the river, and from atop the walls along both sides of the waterway, would have caught their enemy off-guard in a trap. But fortunately for the Persians, their attack was a surprise and they were able to capture the city. Because the city was so large, the citizens located in the central part of town were not aware what had taken place, even though the outer areas of the city had already fallen, **for they were engaged in a festival of dancing and revelry.** This was the account of how Babylon was first conquered.

The account of Herodotus thus verifies that God allowed Cyrus to subdue many nations before him, dry up the mighty waters and enter Babylon's open gates of bronze, all while Belshazzar, their prince, was throwing what would be his last party just as recorded in Daniel chapter 5.

LIKE CYRUS, BELIEVERS ARE CHOSEN BEFOREHAND NOT TO BUILD A TEMPLE OUT OF STONE BUT TO FORM A LIVING TEMPLE

"**Just as He chose us in Him before the foundation of the world**, that we should be holy and without blame before Him in love, **having predestined us to adoption as sons by Jesus** Christ to Himself, according to the good pleasure of His will." Ephesians 1:4-5

"For no other foundation can anyone lay than that which is laid, which is Jesus Christ. Now if anyone builds on this foundation with gold, silver, precious stones, wood, hay, straw, each one's work will become clear; for the Day will declare it, because it will be revealed by fire; and the fire will test each one's work, of what sort it is. If anyone's work which he has built on it endures, he will receive a reward. If anyone's work is burned, he will suffer loss; but he himself will be saved, yet so as through fire. **Do you not know that you are the temple of God and that the Spirit of God dwells in you?**"

1 Corinthians 3:11-16

THE ARK OF THE COVENANT

Throughout history people have had a fascination with finding the ark of the covenant. Even Hollywood, with its adventure packed blockbuster "Raiders of the Lost Ark," captivated the attention of audiences everywhere. It was an exhilarating experience to be taken on a journey with Indiana Jones on his quest for the sacred relic. But unlike the movie, where the Ark was uncovered, in real life its resting place still remains a mystery.

Some believe the ark is hidden somewhere beneath the Temple Mount, in one of the rock carved tunnels that lay underneath. While others believe it was taken out of Israel and carried off to Ethiopia.

Although there are many theories behind where the ark of the covenant currently resides, one thing is certain, archaeology has already proven its existence.

In Jerusalem, the golden roof on the Muslim shrine of the "Dome of the Rock" towers over the site where the Jewish temple once stood. Its foundation is a massive rock on which archaeologists have laid out all the rooms of the old Jewish temple including the Holy of Holies. The Holy of Holies is the room where the ark of the covenant was kept. To this very day a rectangular depression, the same size as the ark of the covenant, can be seen marking where it once stood in the Jewish Temple. The depression measures 4'-4" x 2'-7" (2 ½ cubits x 1 ½ cubits), the exact dimensions of the Ark of the Covenant as recorded in "Exodus 25:10". And it is located right smack dab in the middle of the Holy of Holies.

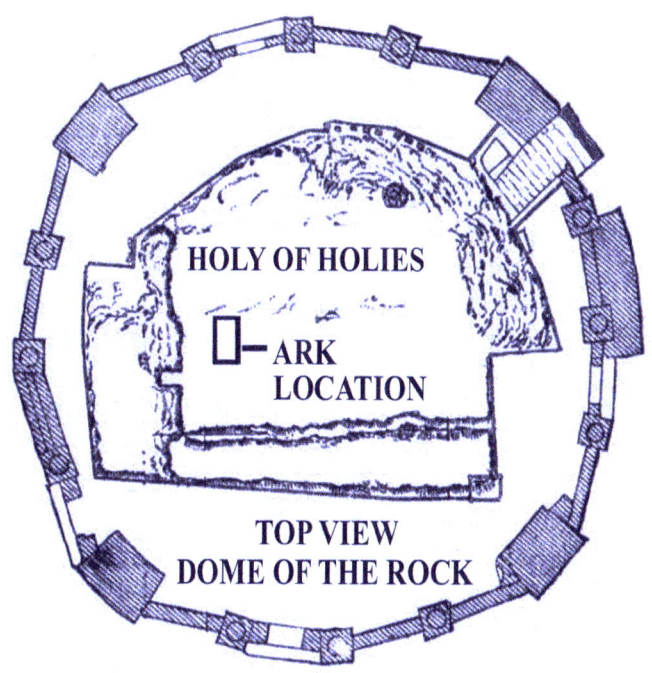

According to Hebrews 9:4, the two tablets of the Ten Commandments were housed in the ark along with a golden pot of manna and Aaron's rod that budded.

The most holy place where the ark was kept was sealed from view by a veil that only the high priest could enter. Once a year he would go behind the curtain into the Holy of Holies to offer a blood sacrifice on the mercy seat of the ark to atone for the sins of the people. The mercy seat was located between the two Cherubim and was where the Lord of Hosts dwelt. (1 Samuel 4:4)

When Jesus was crucified, the veil that separated the Holy of Holies was torn in two, signifying that all people can now come freely into God's presence. No longer is there a need to make an offering for sin, for Jesus our great high priest offered his body as the perfect sacrifice for sins, once for all.

As Hebrews 9:3-15 states: "And behind the second veil, the part of the tabernacle which is called the Holiest of All, which had the golden censer and the ark of the covenant overlaid on all sides with gold, in which were the golden pot that had the manna, Aaron's rod that budded, and the tablets of the covenant; and above it were the cherubim of glory overshadowing the mercy seat. Of these things we cannot now speak in detail.

Now when these things had been thus prepared, the priests always went into the first part of the tabernacle, performing the services. But into the second part the high priest went alone once a year, not without blood, which he offered for himself and for the people's sins until the time of reformation. . . .

But Christ came as High Priest of the good things to come, with the greater and more perfect tabernacle not made with hands, that is, not of this creation. Not with the blood of goats and calves, but with His own blood He entered the Most Holy

Place once for all, having obtained eternal redemption. For if the blood of bulls and goats and the ashes of a heifer, sprinkling the unclean, sanctifies for the purifying of the flesh, how much more shall the blood of Christ, who through the eternal Spirit offered Himself without spot to God, cleanse your conscience from dead works to serve the living God? And for this reason He is the Mediator of the new covenant, by means of death, for the redemption of the transgressions under the first covenant, that those who are called may receive the promise of the eternal inheritance."

Hebrews 10:18-22 says: "Now where there is remission of these, there is no longer an offering for sin.
Therefore, brethren, having boldness to enter the Holiest by the blood of Jesus, by a new and living way which He consecrated for us, through the veil, that is, His flesh, and having a High Priest over the house of God, let us draw near with a true heart in full assurance of faith, having our hearts sprinkled from an evil conscience and our bodies washed with pure water."

The Ark and the Word of God

Deuteronomy 31:8-13: "And the LORD, He is the One who goes before you. He will be with you, He will not leave you nor forsake you; do not fear nor be dismayed."
So Moses wrote this law and delivered it to the priests, the sons of Levi, who bore the **ark of the covenant** of the LORD, and to all the elders of Israel . . . "when all Israel comes to appear before the LORD your God in the place which He chooses, you shall read this law before all Israel in their hearing."

"Gather the people together, men and women and little ones, and the stranger who is within your gates, that they may hear and that they may learn to fear the LORD your God and carefully observe all the words of this law, "and that their children, who have not known it, may hear and learn to fear the LORD your God as long as you live in the land which you cross the Jordan to possess."

Shall the Ark ever be found?

"Then it shall come to pass, when you are multiplied and increased in the land in those days," says the LORD, "that they will say no more, 'The ark of the covenant of the LORD.' It shall not come to mind, nor shall they remember it, nor shall they visit it, nor shall it be made anymore.
"At that time Jerusalem shall be called The Throne of the LORD, and all the nations shall be gathered to it, to the name of the LORD, to Jerusalem. No more shall they follow the dictates of their evil hearts." Jeremiah 3:16-17

Where is the ark?

"Then the temple of God was opened in heaven, and the ark of His covenant was seen in His temple. And there were lightnings, noises, thunderings, an earthquake, and great hail."
Revelation 11:19

The Hand of God Tears the Veil to Threads:

And Jesus cried out again with a loud voice, and yielded up His spirit. Then, behold, **the veil of the temple was torn in two from top to bottom**; and the earth quaked, and the rocks were split, and the graves were opened; and many bodies of the saints who had fallen asleep were raised; and coming out of the graves after His resurrection, they went into the holy city and appeared to many.

So when the centurion and those with him, who were guarding Jesus, saw the earthquake and the things that had happened, they feared greatly, saying, "Truly this was the Son of God!"

Matthew 27:50-54

If you have enjoyed this book, please pass it along to a friend. Jesus said "Freely you have received, freely give."

May the Grace and Peace of the Lord Jesus Christ be with you.

This book as well as our first and third volumes in the Bible Believer's Archaeology series may be ordered at BibleHistory.net as well as from other major online book distributors.

SOURCES:

THE HOLY BIBLE, AUTHOR: THE LORD GOD
Scripture taken from the New King James Version unless noted.

The author and publisher gratefully acknowledges the following resources used in compiling data and illustrations for this publication.

FRONT COVER: Art: "Christ Presented to the People" Illustration for the "Holy Bible" circa 1865 by Artist: Gustave Dore'.

GOD'S GREATEST GIFT: Art: "The face of Jesus" Artist: John Argubright
Copyright © 1997 John Argubright.

CHAPTER #1: "THE BIRTH OF JESUS"

Origen - Against Celsus, Volume I, Chapter 51.
(Origen account of the cave where Jesus was born)

Ambrosius Macrobius "Saturnalia Book 2, Chapter 4:11"
Roman writer around 430 A.D. (Quotes Caesar Augustus as saying "I'd rather be Herod's pig than his son.)

Evidence That Demands a Verdict - Volume 1, Author: Josh Mcdowell
ISBN 0-918956-46-3
pg.115-116 Quotes from Ignatius, Aristides and Justin Martyr on the virgin birth.

Josephus The Essential Writings, Author: Paul L. Maier, ISBN 0-8254-2963-3
Pg 252 (Herod's death and the Hippodrome account.)

Radio Ministry: Hope for Today, Speaker David Hocking Cassette Message #2025: Luke 2:1-14 (Tower of the Flock and Migdal Eder information.)

Artwork:' Wisemen From the East' Illustrated in "The Illuminated Bible Containing the Old and New Testaments" (1846) pg.3 Publisher: Harper and Brothers.

Artwork:'The Good Shepherd' Illustrated in "The Parables of our Lord and Saviour Jesus Christ" (1864) Illustrated by John Everett Millais, Engraved by the Dalziel brothers. Publisher: Routledge, Warne and Routledge.

CHAPTER #2: "QUIRINIUS"

Res Gestae - "The Deeds of Augustus"
Res Gestae 10: Account of Quirinius as consul in 12 B.C.
Res Gestae 8: Augustus held three census to count Roman citizens in 28 B.C., 14 B.C. and 8 B.C.
Res Gestae, 6.35 It is important to note that in these census accounts they were not counting non Romans as citizens, such as those in Judea. So these dates in all likelihood had nothing to do with the Biblical census.
In 2 B.C. Caesar wrote that "while I was administering my thirteenth consulship the Senate and the equestrian order and the entire Roman people gave me the title Father of my country and decreed that this title should be inscribed upon the vestibule of my house and in the senate-house and in the Forum Augustum beneath the quadriga erected in my honour by decree of the senate."

Suetonius, *Life of Augustus*, 58, also mentions this title "Father of thy country" given to Augustus. In 59-60 it states: "Many of the provinces, in addition to temples and altars, established quinquennial games (games every five years) in his honour in almost every one of their towns. His friends and allies among the kings each in his own realm founded a city called Caesarea. This event in 2 B.C. may have led Herod to place a large Roman Golden Eagle on a gate of the Temple in Jerusalem to honor Caesar right before his death which probably occured early in 1 B.C. This is recorded by Josephus in Antiquities Book 17 Chapter 6. It also goes hand in hand with Josephus stating that his allies, one being Phillip, who renamed the city of Panias to Caesarea Phillipi shortly after Herod Death. (Note: Herod the Great earlier built another Caesarea, Caesarea Maritime, which would later become the Roman governing center of Judea.

Tacitus Annals:
Book 1 Chapter 3: Account of Gaius wounded in Armenia.
Records the tribute of Tiberius Caesar to Quirinius before the Senate in 22 A.D.
Book 2 Chapter 4: Account of Gaius Caesar appointment to Armenia.
Book 3 Chapter 48: Records the tribute of Tiberius Caesar to Quirinius before the Senate in 22 A.D. Mentions Quirinius as advisor to Caius Caesar as well as a messenger of Rome to Tiberius who was exiled at Rhodes. Earlier was consul under Augustus and garnered fame by capturing the Homonadensian strongholds beyond the Cilician frontier earning the insignia of triumph. Also mentioned as being an active servant and intrepid soldier.

Lives of the Twelve Caesars - Tiberius XLIX - by Suetonius mentions Quirinius held the title of consul.

Inscriptiones Latinae Selectae (ILS-2683) by Herman Dessau–
Corpus Inscriptionum Latinarum (CIL3-6687)
Aemillius Secundus Inscription mentioning Quirinius as legate of Syria and ordering a census. English translation based on translation from 'Documents Illustrating the reigns of Augustus and Tiberius collected by V. Ehrenberg & A.H.M. Jones p.73

Inscriptiones Latinae Selectae (ILS9502 & 9503)
L'Annee Epigrahique (AE1913, 0235 and AE1914, 0260)
Both inscriptions mention Quirinius.

Inscriptiones Latinae Selectae (ILS918) & Corpus Inscriptionum Latinarum (CIL14-03613) - although no specific man is mentioned in the inscription, the early translators attributed the deeds to be that of Quirinius.

Jewish Antiquities by Josephus :
Book 14: 271-176 Cassius taxes Judea from Syria.
Book 15: 267: Herod introduced pagan games into Judea very early during his reign. He built a theater in Jerusalem. So since Caesar later held games in 2 B.C. along with being named "Father of his country" by the Roman senate. This is probably the date at which Herod placed a Roman Eagle on the Temple gate.
Book 16: 150-170 Herod's taxing of the people.
Book 17 Chapter 2: Account of pharisees refusing to take an oath of good will to Caesar and to that of Herod's government which was required of all Israel.
Book 17:146 Herod placed a large golden eagle on the Temple gate and Herod's death.
Book 17:188-193 Herod's payment to Caesar of 10 million.
Book 17:200 - The speech of Archelaus after Herod's death and the peoples cry for their taxes to be reduced.

Book 17 Chapter 9 also mentions that when a dispute over who should rule over the deceased King Herod's territories. One of the people he sought an opinion from was his adopted son Caius Caesar who would became legate in Syria in 1 B.C. or 1 A.D. If Herod died in 1 B.C. it would correspond with Caius being installed as legate to that region.
Book 17 Chapter 13: Cyrenius sent by Caesar to confiscate Archelaus property and to take account of the peoples belongings in Syria.
Book 18 Chapter 1: Quirinius came into Syria with a few others to administer that nation, Cyrenius also came into Judea to take account of their substance as well of to dispose of the estate of Archelaus. Archelaus (Matthew 2:22) ruled for 10 years according to Josephus in Antiquities Book 17, So if Herod died in 1 B.C. this would be 9 A.D. for the date of the death of Archelaus.
Book 18 Chapter 2: The Jewish revolt against the taxation by Quirinius. Also Quirinius appoints Annas as High Priest at the end of this taxation. Coponius, who was sent along with Cyrenius, who was exercising the office of procurator of Judea at this time.

Bible: Luke 3:1 States John the Baptist began his ministry in the fifteenth year of Tiberius Caesar (28 A.D.). Luke 3:23 states that at this time Jesus began his ministry when he was about thirty, If He was 30 this would place the date of his birth in 2 B.C. and would mean that Herod would have died in the spring of 1 B.C. right before Passover according to Josephus. But one must be cautious because the Bible uses the phrase "about thirty" which could mean that he could have been anywhere between his late twenties and early thirties.

Article: "When was Jesus Born" December 2006 Article, Author: David Hocking Evidence for Jesus born in 2 B.C.

Irenaeus, Against Heresies, Anti-Nicene Fathers Volume 1
Book III.xxi.3   Robers and Donaldson - Eerdmans 1885
Irenaeus states: "Our Lord was born about the 41rst year of the reign of Augustus" Since Augustus was first given Imperium powers by the Roman Senate as well as becoming a Consul in 43 B.C., this would place the census at 2 B.C.

Tertullian , An Answer to the Jews, Ante-Nicene Fathers, Volume III.
Part I, vii, 8 mentions that Augustus began to reign 41 years before the birth of Christ. And 28 years after the death of Cleopatra who died in 30 B.C. therefore also giving a date of 2 B.C. for the census.

Josephus Re-Examined: Unraveling the Twenty-Second Year of Tiberius, in Chronos, Kairos, Christos II, Author: David W. Beyer, edited by E. Jerry Vardaman, Macon: Mercer University Press, 1998, ISBN 0-86554-582-0 pg. 85
Argument for 1 B.C. date of Herod's Death as well as 2 B.C. date for Christ's birth as held by the church historians Tertullian, Origen and Eusibius as well inferred by Josephus. According to his research most Josephus manuscripts dated prior to 1544 A.D. In Jewish Antiquities Book 18 Section 106, have Phillip (Herod's son) dying in the 22nd year of Tiberius, which would be 35/36 A.D. and he ruled for 37 years. Thus giving a date of 1 B.C. or 2 B.C. as for when he was appointed Tetrarch right after Herod's death.

The Star that Astonished the world, Author Ernest L. Martin. Chapter 8 makes the case for a Lunar Eclipse account recorded in Josephus Antiquities Book 17 Chapter 6 that occurred some time before Herod's death as most likely the total lunar Eclipse that occurred in mid January of 1 B.C. allowing time for the events of Herod's illness, death and funeral before the Passover that year.

DVD: The Star of Bethlehem - Rick Larson states the earliest copies of Josephus before 1544 A.D. infer a date of 1 B.C. for the date of Herod's death.

Artwork: Pen and Ink Reproduction of Inscriptiones Latinae Selectae #9502 mentioning Quirinius based upon G.L. Cheesman photo from his book "The Family of Caristanii at Antioch Pisidia." Illustrator: John Argubright - Copyright © 2000

CHAPTER #3: "THE CLEANSING OF THE TEMPLE"

Smiths Bible Dictionary, Author: William Smith as published by Fleming H. Revell Co. & Spire Books. Pg.240 List of High Priests mentioned from Aaron to the High priests of the first century.

Antiquities of the Jews, By the historian Josephus, Book 20 - Chapter 9: Account of Ananus the younger, Also a list of Jewish High priests from Aaron onward.

Quotes from the Talmud: Megillah 13b, 29a-b: Shekel Cycle mention of Money changers in the temple at Passover.

Quote from Tosefta, Menahoth 13.21 on woes to the first century high priests.

The Life and Times of Jesus the Messiah by Alfred Erdersheim
Rosh haShannah 31 a,b speaks of the "Bazaars of the Sons of Annas."

Artwork: "The cleansing of the Temple" Illustrated in "The Illuminated Bible Containing the Old and New Testaments" (1846) pg.50 Pub. Harper and Brothers.

CHAPTER #4: "PONTIUS PILATE"

Artwork:'Jesus presented to the people' Illustrated in "Art and Music - Childcraft Volume 13. (1939) Publisher: Quarrie Corp.

Artwork:'Jesus before Pilate' Illustrated in Cassell's Illuminated Family Bible Vol. 4 from Matthew to Revelation pg.85, Publisher: Cassell, Petter & Calpin (1860)

Evidence That Demands a Verdict (Vol.1) Author: Josh Mcdowell
ISBN 0-918956-46-3, pg.81-82 Quotes from Tacitus Annals XV.44 concerning Pilate putting Christ to death.

The Jewish War by Josephus, 2.175-177, Pilate and the construction of the aqueduct.

Josephus The Essential Writings, Author: Paul L. Maier ISBN 0-8254-2964-1 pg. 264 Account of Pilate and the aqueduct incident.

The Works of Philo: Complete and Unabridged, Author: C.D. Younge
ISBN 0-9435-7593-1 The Embassy of Gaius 299-305.

CHAPTER #5: "THE CRUCIFIED PROPHET"

Lucian, The Death of Peregrine, 11–13, in The Works of Lucian of Samosata, translated by F.G. Fowler and H.W. Fowler, 4 vols. (Oxford:Clarendon, 1949), vol4.

Artwork: Illustration of "The Christ," a sculpture by Francois Rude Illustrated in the 'Encyclopedia of Art-Vol. 1&2 (1937) Author: Davidson and Gerry Publisher: Garden City Publishing Company, Inc.

CHAPTER #6: "AQUILA AND PRISCILLA FLEE ROME"

The New Testament Documents ISBN 0-85110-307-3
Author: F.F. Bruce pg.118 Suetonius quote from (Life of Claudius XXV.4).

Letter of Claudius [P.London 1912] (from *Select Papyri* II [Loeb Classical Library] (ed. A.S.Hunt and G.C. Edgar) (1934), pp. 78-89, adapted.)

Artwork: "Paul visiting Aquila and Priscilla in Corinth." Illustrated in 'The New Testament - A Pictorial Archive from Nineteenth Century Sources - 311 Copyright-Free Illustrations', Edited by Don Rice, Publisher: Dover Publications.

CHAPTER #7: "THE FAMINE OF ACTS CHAPTER 11"

The Anglo-Saxon Chronicles: Britannia.com - history department.

The MacArthur Study Bible: pg.1654, Published by Thomas Nelson
The plague of Acts 11 recorded by Tacitus, Seutonius and Josephus AD 45-46.

Life of Claudius by Seutonius, chapter 18, Source: Internet Ancient History Sourcebook - Fordham.edu, Scarcity of food for several years due to bad crops.

Antiquities of the Jews by Josephus, Chapter 20 1.3-2.5
Queen Helena and the Famine.

Tacitus Annals 11:4, Source from classics.mit.edu
Account of a similar prophetic vision.

Artwork: "Joseph of Arimathea and others taking down the body of Jesus from the cross" Illustrated in Cassell's Illuminated Family Bible Vol. 4 from Matthew to Revelation pg.89, Publisher: Cassell, Petter & Calpin (1860).

CHAPTER #8: "THE MARTYRS"

The New Testament Documents, Are They Reliable? ISBN #0-85110-307-3
Author: F.F. Bruce pg.119 Pliny the Younger Quote.

Evidence that Demands a Verdict ISBN 0-918956-46-3
Author: Josh Mcdowell pg. 83 Pliny the Younger and Suetonius info.

Pliny Letters 10.96-97: Letters from Pliny to the Emperor Trajan and Trajan's reply to Pliny.

Artwork: "The Stoning of Stephen" Illustrated in Cassell's Illuminated Family Bibe Vol. 4 from Matthew to Revelation pg.112, Publisher: Cassell, Petter & Calpin (1860)

CHAPTER #9: "ACTS 21 - THE EGYPTIAN"

Josephus: Antiquities of the Jews 20 Chapter 8 Section 5 (The Jewish War 2 Chapter 13 Section 5) The Egyptian Account.

Josephus The Essential Writings, ISBN 0-8254-2963-3 Author : Paul Maier

Artwork: "Soldiers bringing Paul into the barracks" Illustrated in "The Child's Bible being a Consecutive Arrangement of the Bible" (1884)
Author: Dr. J.H. Vincent, Publisher: Cassell and Company.

Artwork: "Paul before Felix and Drusilla" Illustrated in "The Child's Bible being a Consecutive Arrangement of the Bible" (1884)
Author: Dr. J.H. Vincent, Publisher: Cassell and Company.

CHAPTER #10: "THE WALL SEPARATING JEWS AND GENTILES"

The Stones Cry Out, ISBN 1-56507-640-0, Author: Randall Price
Page 317 Soreg inscription info.

Antiquities of the Jews, Historian: Josephus
Chapter 15.417 mentions warning inscription.

The New Testament Documents - Are they Reliable? ISBN 0-85110-307-3
Author: F.F. Bruce, Pages 93-94 Information on warning inscription.

Artwork: Pen and Ink reproduction of the "Soreg Inscription"
Illustrator: John Argubright - Copyright © 2000.

CHAPTER #11: "ADAM, THE FLOOD AND THE TOWER OF BABEL"

The Bible in the British Museum, Interpreting the Evidence
Author: T.C Mitchell, ISBN #0-8091-4292-9
pg.24 Temptation Seal,
pg 25 Ziggurat at UR.
pg 89 Cylinder of Nabonidus mentioning Belshazzar and the rebuilt tower at Ur.

Ancient Near Eastern Texts Relating to the Old Testament
Author James Pritchard, ISBN 0-691-03503-2
pg.243 & 247 Egyptian accounts mentioning the land of Shinar.
pg.265 The Sumerian king list mentioning that a flood swept over the earth and that in Kish (Cush) the first kingdom was restored. Also mentions the Elamites.
pg.44 Sumerian account found at Nippur concerning a flood that destroyed mankind.
Pg,270-271 A temple tower built by Hammurabi, his son also mentions a temple tower.
Pg.93-95 Gilgamesh Epic with account similar to that of the Bible's.
Pg..274 Mention of the city of Ashur on inscription dating back to Shamshi-Adad I, 1726-1694 B.C.
Pg.165 Mention of the city of Nineveh in Hammurabi code who ruled between 1728-1686 B.C.
Pg.605 Mention of the cities of Ashur, Nineveh and Calah together by Esarhaddon king of Assyria around 680-669 B.C.

The Ancient Near East - Volume 2, A new Anthology of Texts and Pictures. James Pritchard, ISBN 0-691-00209-6, Pg.100 Mention of Calah by Ashurnasirpal II.

British Museum website: Mentions that Nebuchadnezzar rebuilt the ziggurat tower called Entemenanki.

The Chaldean Account of Genesis containing the Description of the Creation . . ,

Author: George Smith, Publisher Scribner & Armstrong 1876, pg 160-162, Assyrian fragments mentioning the Tower of Babel account. Internet text at http://historical.library.cornell.edu. "The Cornell Library of Historical Monographs."

According to Dr. Paul Collins, Curator (Later Mesopotamia) Department of the Ancient Near East of The British Museum (2006): "Smith's translation comes from a fragmentary cuneiform tablet discovered at Nineveh by Austen Henry Layard and now in the British Museum (registration number K.3657). In 1993 it was recognized that another fragment (Rm.114) belonged to the same tablet and the two pieces were joined. Alas, the second fragment is equally fragmentary and has not yet been fully translated or published."

Oriental Museum's photo collection from Mesopotamia of ziggurats found at Khorsabad Tepe Gawra, Nimrud (Calah = Kalhu), Assur, Aqarquf (one of the highest left standing) Sippar, Kish, Borsippa, Nippur, Uruk, UR (rebuilt by Nabonidus, location of Belshazzar inscription), and Eridu.
http://oi.uchicago.edu/OI/IS/SANDERS/PHOTOS/arch_site_photos.html (2006)

Royal Inscription of Assurnasirpal (MS711) dated from Assyria (883-859 B.C.) and states "Calah I restored." (The National Library of Norway) The Schoyen Collection http://www.nb.no/baser/schoyen/4/4.2/423.html (2006)

Illustrated Bible Dictionary and Treasury of Bible History. Author Matthew George Easton. Publisher; Nelson and Sons (1894). Pg, 134 Illustration of the Chaldean account of the Tower of Babel, British Museum number K.3657

Artwork: Partial Reproduction of "The Dove sent forth from the Ark - Genesis 8:11" Illustration for the "Holy Bible" circa 1865 by Artist: Gustave Dore'

Artwork: "The Tower of Babel - Genesis 11:4" Illustration for the "Holy Bible" circa 1865 by Artist: Gustave Dore'. Also illustrated in "Dore' Bible Illustrations" (1891) Artist: Gustave Dore', Publisher: Bedford Clarke Publishers.

Artwork: "Flood artifact - Epic of Gilgamesh" Illustrated in ""Virgil's Aenid" (1944) Author: John Dryden, Artist Carlotta Petrina, Publisher: Heritage Press. Also photographed in 'Book of History Volume 4 0" (The Near East Section) pg.1643, publisher: Grolier Society.

Artwork: "Temptation Seal" Illustrated in "The Chaldean Account of Genesis containing the Description of the Creation ..." (1876) pg.91 Author George Smith of the Oriental Department of the British Museum, Publisher: Scribner, Armstrong & Company.

Artwork: "Tower of Babel Fragment - British Museum K3657" Illustrated in "The Seven Tablets of Creation - Luzac's Semetic Text and Translation Series Vol. XIII" (1902) Edited by L.W. King - Assistant in the Department of Egyptian and Assyrian Antiquities of the British Museum. Publisher: Luzac anc Company.

CHAPTER #12: "THE ROCK CITY"

Title: Audio cassette message "How does God show his Love?" Side 2 (Malachi 1:1-15) message 7007- Solid Rock Radio - Delivered by Bible teacher David Hocking

Josephus "Antiquities of the Jews" Book 13, Chapter 9:1
Mention of Hycranus defeat of the Idumeans, Josephus Antiquities 13:254, W 1:62

The MacArthur Study Bible: Pg.1278, Publisher Thomas Nelson (notes on Amos 1:11-12), pg.1288-1289 Notes on Obadiah.

Hymn: A mighty fortress is our God, Author & Composer: Martin Luther.

Biblical prophecies concerning Edom: Isaiah 34:5-16 , 62:11-63:8 , Jer 49:7-22, Amos 1:11-12, Ezekiel 35, Malachi 1:2-4, Ezekiel 25:14.

Teman: the grandson of Esau Gen 36:11 after whom this town in northern Edom was named. Bozrah: A fortress city of Northern Edom, about 35 mi. N of Petra. source: see pg. 1278 The MacArthur Study Bible.

Artwork: "View of narrow canyon entrance to Petra" Illustrated in "Aloha around the World" (1923) Author: Karl Vogel, Publisher: G.P. Putnam and Sons.

Artwork: "The ancient city of Petra" Illustrated in "Bellezze D' Italia: La Citta Del Vaticano" (1930), Author:Mario Giordano. Publisher: Edizioni Italia Artistica.

CHAPTER #13: "LOT'S DESCENDANTS"

Biblical Archaeology Review March/April 1999 Vol.25 No.2
Pg.46-49 Ammonite Seals.

The Ancient Near East: Volume 1 An Anthology of Text and Pictures- Princeton University Press edited by James Pritchard, ISBN 0-691-00200-2
pg.190 mention of Ahab king of Israel and Basa son of Ruhubi from Ammon.

The Revell Bible Dictionary ISBN 0-8007-1594-2
pg.56 limestone statue head of an Ammorite king dated during the time frame of Jehoshaphat. pg.422 Gedaliah seal picture (British Museum, London).

Artwork: 'Gedaliah seal' pen and ink reproduction, Illustrator: John Argubright Copyright © 2013

Artwork: Pen and ink reproduction of Rembrandt's 'Lot's departure from Sodom' Illustrator: John Argubright - Copyright © 2000

CHAPTER #14: "JEHU & HAZAEL"

Ancient Near Eastern Texts Relating to the Old Testament. James Pritchard
pg.280 Hazael seizes the throne account.
pg.281 Black Obelisk account of Jehu giving tribute to Shalmaneser III.

Artwork: "Black Obelisk showing Jehu giving tribute to Shalmaneser" Illustrated in "History of the World - Vol.1" (1909) Author: J.C. Ridpath, Publisher: Jones Brother Publishing.

CHAPTER #15: "KING UZZIAH"

Halley's Bible Handbook - Author: Henry H. Halley, ISBN: 0-310-25720-4
Pg.223-224 Uzziah inscription.

Biblical Archaeology Review Nov/Dec 1995
Biblical Archaeology Review Jul/Aug 2001

Journal of Biblical Literature - Vol 28, No. 2 1909 pg.182-199
Azariah of Judah and Tiglath Pileaser III by author Howell M. Haydn
Published by The Society of Biblical Literature.
Texts known as III R 9, No.1, No. 2, No. 3 May refer to Azariah of Judah, scholars disagree over this artifact.

Ancient Near Eastern Texts Relating to the Old Testament. James Pritchard pg.282 Mention of Tiglath-Pileaser receiving tribute from Azriau of Iuda, possibly Azariah of Judah, though scholars disagree over the translation.

Artwork: Pen and Ink Reproduction of the "Uzziah burial inscription"
Illustrator: John Argubright - Copyright © 2000

CHAPTER #16: "AHAZ, KING OF JUDAH"

Halley's Bible Handbook - Author: Henry H. Halley, ISBN: 0-310-25720-4
Pg.224 Ahaz and Tiglath-Pileser inscriptions.

The Ancient Near East - Volume 1 - An Anthology of Texts and Pictures Edited by James B. Pritchard ISBN 0-691-00200-2
pg.193 Tiglath-Pileser III Campaigns against Syria and Israel. (ANET 282)

Ahaz Artifact -British Museum WAK 3751.

Biblical Archaeology Review - May/June 1998 pg.54-56

CHAPTER #17: "SARGON, KING OF ASSYRIA"

Dare to be a Daniel, author David Hocking, ISBN 0-939497-26-3 Promise publishing pg.3-4 information on Sargon.

The Ancient Near East, Volume 1 An Anthology of Texts and Pictures Edited by James B. Pritchard, Princeton University Press ISBN 0-691-00200-2
Pg.195 Sargon Inscription.

Ancient Near Eastern Texts Relating to the Old Testament. James Pritchard pg.284-285 Mention of Sargon's attack on Samaria and Israel, as well as Ashdod and Ashdod's alliance with Egypt, Also mentions Egypt and Ethiopia as fearing Assyria.

The Schoyen Collection
Royal Inscription of Sargon - MS 2368 Nimrud Prism IV 25-41
Mentions conquest of Bit-Humriya (House of Omri) Israel.

Photograph of winged bull from Sargon's palace at Dur-Sharrukin ('the fortress of Sargon'), known today as Khorsabad, can be found at the British museum's website.

Artwork: "Winged bull from Sargon's palace" Illustrated in "Styles of Ornament" (1928) Author: Alexander Spletz, Publisher: Grosset and Dunlap.

CHAPTER #18: "MANASSEH, SON OF HEZEKIAH"

The Revell Bible Dictionary by Fleming H Revell, ISBN 0-8007-1594-2 pg. 667 Photograph of clay prism located in the British Museum.

The Word of God: 2Kings 21:1-18 / 2 Chr 33:1-20

A Repentance Bible Study:
Luke 13:3, Acts 2:38, Acts 3:19, Acts 17:30, Luke 24:47
Acts 5:31, Acts 26:20 2, Corinthians 7:9-11, Romans 2:4

Artwork: "Manasseh being led into captivity" Illustrated in: "Art and Music- Childcraft Vol. 13" (1939) Publisher: Quarrie Corp.

Artwork: Esarhaddon Prism mentioning "Manasseh King of Judah" ANET 291 Modified Taylor Prism illustration of artifact to look like the Esarhaddon Prism, Illustrated in 'Book of History Volume 4 0" (The Near East Section) pg.1616, publisher: Grolier Society.

"Ancient Near Eastern Texts - Relating to the Old Testament" Edited by James B. Pritchard
pg. 291 (Manasseh mentioned in records from the Assyrian king Esarhaddon 680-669 B.C.)
Pg. 290 Inscription "Esarhaddon....king of Assyria, governor of Babylon."
Pg. 293 Esarhaddon mentions he attacked Egypt and Ethiopia and took many captives.

Another inscription from Esarhaddon reads: "Babylon I built anew, I enlarged it, I raised it aloft, I made it magnificent.

CHAPTER #19: "JEREMIAH"S ENEMY"

Biblical Archaeology Review, January/February 2006 pg.26 Jehucal Seal.

Ancient Near Eastern Texts Relating to the Old Testament. James Pritchard
pg.322 Lachish letter IX mentioning Shelemiah, pg.322 Lachish letter VIII mentions Nedabiah, who may have been Zedekiah's nephew as listed in 1Chronicles 3:18.

Artwork: Pen and Ink Reproduction of the "Jehucal son of Shelemiah" seal
Illustrator: John Argubright - Copyright © 2006

Artwork: Pen and Ink Reproduction of the "Gedaliah son of Pushhur" seal
Illustrator: John Argubright - Copyright © 2008

Artwork: "Jeremiah being rescued from the well" Illustrated in: "Art and Music - Childcraft Vol. 13" (1939) Publisher: Quarrie Corp.

CHAPTER #20: "KING CYRUS OF PERSIA"

The Ancient Near East, Author: James B. Pritchard, pg.207-208 Cyrus Decree.

The history of Herodotus - Book 1, Author: Herodotus written 440 B.C. Translation by George Rawlinson. Cyrus Account.

Artwork: "Tomb of King Cyrus" Illustrated in "International Cyclopaedia Vol. XI, (1892) Author: H.T. Peck, Publisher: Dodd, Mead and Company.

Artwork: "Cyrus Cylinder" Illustrated in "Popular and Critical Bible Encyclopedia Vol.1, (1910) Author: S.Fallows, Publisher: Howard Severance Company.

CHAPTER #21: "THE ARK OF THE COVENANT"

Biblical Archaeology Review, Jan/Feb 1996 Issue
Pg.46-55 "The Ark of the Covenant in Solomon's Temple."

The Stones Cry Out, Author: Randall Price ISBN#1-56507-640-0
Pg.211-219 "Has archaeology found the place of the ark?"

Artwork: Partial reproduction of 'The Israelites Crossing the Jordan' Artist: Julius Schnorr von Carolsfeld Illustrated in "Bible in Bildern" Circa 1851-1860.

Artwork: Illustration of the top view looking down from the Dome of the Rock. Original Illustration was modified to show the location of the impression where the ark of the covenant rested. Original illustration taken from Scribner's Monthly - Volume 11, December 1875 Article: "The site of Solomon's Temple Discovered" pg.265, Author: Scribner and Company, Publisher: Francis Hart and Company.

Artwork: partial reproduction of 'The Curtain of the Temple Torn' Artist: Henry Felix Emmanual Philippoteaux - Circa 1840-1880.

REAR COVER: Illustration: Partial reproduction of the crucifixion from Rembrandt's "The two criminals" Artist: Rembrandt.

www.ingramcontent.com/pod-product-compliance
Lightning Source LLC
Chambersburg PA
CBHW072338300426
44109CB00042B/1737